The
SECRET HISTORY
of
OXFORD

The
SECRET HISTORY
of
OXFORD

Paul Sullivan

The
History
Press

For Jay, Jan and Theo

First published 2013

The History Press
The Mill, Brimscombe Port
Stroud, Gloucestershire, GL5 2QG
www.thehistorypress.co.uk

British Library Cataloguing in Publication Data.
A catalogue record for this book is available from the British Library.

ISBN 978 0 7524 9956 7

Typesetting and origination by The History Press
Printed in Great Britain

Contents

Acknowledgements

Thanks to:

Jan Sullivan for the fun we had exploring, photographing and eating all-day breakfasts

Anthea Davies for providing the perfect hideaway to sort out my notes

Magda Bezdekova for ferrying me around and looking after us all

Pavel Bezdek for invaluable research material

Heather Robbins for the May Morning pics

Jacqui Julier at New College for the unicorn information

Andrew Salmon of Paynes the silversmiths for trying to find the owner of the watch dog

The good folk of Buxton for comradeship, art and beer

Cate Ludlow and Naomi Reynolds at The History Press for editing out the bad bits

Preface

On my first day as a resident in Oxford, I caught a bus to the city centre and stood, lost but intrigued, at St Frideswide's Square. Getting my bearings from a map, I decided to visit the castle, from which vantage point I would plan my raid on the college-riddled treasure trove beyond Carfax.

Before I had taken a single step I was, to my great surprise, hailed by Graham Clark, a friend from my previous hometown of Buxton. I'd no idea he was in the city, but it turned out he was staying on a friend's narrow boat at Osney Marina. I accompanied him to the river, and during my brief visit the boat's owner, Tom Troscianko, introduced us to several interesting things in addition to his splendid floating home – great local beer, the last remains of Osney Abbey at the ruined mill, The Kite public house on Mill Street, the priceless old fiddle in the Ashmolean Museum, and the American signal crayfish that infest the rivers in Oxford.

This red-clawed mini lobster is far from home and far from welcome. It infects the native white-clawed crayfish with 'crayfish plague', undermines riverbanks with its burrows, and generally messes up the grumpy ecosystem. And yet it is illegal to interfere with crayfish: they cannot be moved, caught for consumption or used as bait without a license. The law is obtuse: if one is netted by mistake, you are not allowed to throw it back and nor can you eat it. You can probably guess what Tom's response to the dilemma was.

This was my first detour into Oxford secrets, crammed into my first hour in the city. That detour has continued ever since. I finally made it to the castle about a year after setting out in its general direction.

During the research for this book, I learned from Graham that Tom had died in his sleep in Amsterdam, on his way to a conference in Germany. I recalled that first day at Osney Marina – the first chapter of my own secret Oxford – and realised that without that first detour, I wouldn't be writing this. So, thanks to Graham, Tom, and everyone else who's kept me from the straight path.

Chapter One

A Brief History
of Oxford

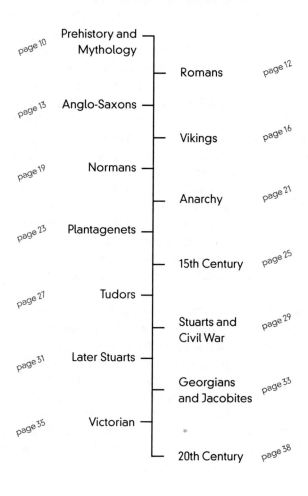

Oxford's greatest secret, and one which it still refuses to whisper to the hapless historian, concerns the foundation of the city and its university. Over the years there have been various theories, some comical, some plausible, all – appropriately enough – without foundation.

The most ambitious investigators have pinned their hopes on prehistory. Three generations after the fall of Troy in 1200 BC, Brutus, a descendent of King Priam of Troy, founded Britain. His three brothers did equally well, founding proto-versions of France, Germany and Rome. Brutus, carrying a cargo of Athenian philosophers, established a university at Greeklade (Cricklade in Wiltshire, alternatively Lechlade in Gloucestershire), later moving it to the site now occupied by Oxford. The position was so beautiful that they named it *Bellositum* (lovely place), root of the later name 'Beaumont', Oxford's royal twelfth-century palace.

Mythology names Mempric (variously spelt Memphric, Menbriz, Membyr or Mempricius), great-grandson of King Brutus, as actual founder of the city. Having murdered his brother Malin at a banquet in order to silence the opposition, he became the terror of the island, killing all political rivals, and bringing dishonour to the royal Trojan line by forsaking his Queen in favour of young men. Founding Oxford (Caer Mempric) was his one good deed. Around 1009 BC Mempric went hunting with his courtiers; they abandoned him in a forest, where he was eaten by wolves. The grisly site was named Wolvercote, which later became an Oxford suburb.

In the reign of King Arthur the city was known as Caer Bosso, the City of Bosso. This 'Big Boss' was a local chieftain who attended the coronation of King Arthur at Caerleon in AD 516. He probably sprang fully formed from the Roman town name Bos Vadum (see next page): early historians felt no qualms about inventing a character to explain a place-name. Bosso is also referred to as *Bosso of Rydychen*, the latter element being a British word translating as 'Oxen-ford'. It's all a bit of a mess, but is tantalisingly in line with a strand of almost-plausible tradition that places the university's foundation a few decades before St Augustine brought Christianity to Saxon England in AD 595.

Whether tantalising or farcical, these are the stories that rise to the surface when the Dark Ages refuse to give up their secrets.

The Romans

Some early historians, rejecting the Brutus story, nominated semi-mythical Romano-British king Arviragus as the founder of the university. The shadowy historical Arviragus, clearly a British chieftain of some importance, lived during the reign of Roman Emperor Domitian (AD 81–96), but legend places him in the reign of Emperor Claudius (AD 41–54). He is said to have married the latter's daughter and ruled as British king under Rome's benevolent eye. He rebuilt several war-torn cities, including Oxford, establishing its university for good measure. The city was known as *Bos Vadum*.

In the mid-first century AD the Roman general Aulus Plautus levelled a few British cities during the Roman conquest. Legend says that Bos Vadum was one of them; but the historical record is silent on the matter.

It seems safe to say that the Romans didn't actually found Oxford at all, but had small settlements in the immediate vicinity, north and east of the present city centre. Remains of a first-century AD wall have been unearthed at the site of the Churchill Kilns, at the Churchill Hospital. Human and dog bones were discovered in the foundations, possibly placed there as sacrificial offerings.

This same site has also yielded the earliest named human in these parts: Tamesibugus. A fragment of Churchill pottery, on display in The Museum of Oxford, bears the legend '*TAMESIBUGUS FECIT*' translating as 'Thames-dweller made this'. Perhaps he was executed and buried, with his dog, after being found guilty of scrawling graffiti on pottery – a theory no sillier than some of those on the previous page.

The Anglo-Saxons

We're still in the realms of mythology when King Alfred the Great (AD 849–899) walks dejectedly through the ruins of Oxenford. Appalled at the damage to learning brought about by the previous century of Saxon versus Dane warfare, he determines to build – some say rebuild – a university in Oxford. To this end he establishes three new university halls in 886, and re-erects several academic halls.

Until the nineteenth century, Oxonians were proud to state that King Alfred founded Oxford University in the year 877. They first made the connection in 1387, when University College tried to ingratiate King Richard II by pointing out that its founder was his famous Saxon predecessor. (The college also claimed that the Venerable Bede had studied there ... even though the famous monastic scholar died more than 100 years before Alfred was born.)

The essence of it is certainly believable – Alfred was a great patron of learning, and actively worked to bring teachers and books into his battered kingdom. There is, however, no direct evidence that he was active in Oxford. The city is not mentioned in any surviving document of the time, although a tantalising 'Orsnaford' is captured on some coins of the period – almost a typo for 'Oxnaford', the Saxon name for the city, and equally close to 'Osney' (the name of the pre-Oxford Abbey near the modern Osney Marina in the city).

Back with real history, archaeology indicates that the sites of local Roman occupation, based around the

St Michael's, Oxford's oldest surviving building.

Churchill Kilns and Headington, were encompassed by a royal estate in the pre-Alfredian Saxon era. A mere 8 miles south, St Birinus was installed as Bishop of Dorchester in the 630s, the small town being one of the most important Christian bases in the island.

St Frideswide (AD 650–727) is said to have founded a priory on the site now occupied by Christ Church College. She is also associated with a long-gone nunnery at neighbouring Binsey. Oxford seems to have been around in all but name.

In the year 912 we get, at last, the first definite mention of Oxford: 'This year died Æthered ealdorman of the Mercians, and King Edward took possession of London and Oxford and of all the lands which owed obedience thereto.'

Oxford was clearly an established city; otherwise Æthered would have had nothing to take possession of. This gives us a foundation in the reign of King Alfred's son, Edward the Elder (AD 899-912), at the very latest, but probably much earlier (he said, returning to those fruitless circles).

Oxford's oldest surviving building dates from the late Saxon period – the mid-eleventh century St Michael's Church tower. A mix of the holy and the secular, the structure was formerly attached to the city's Bocardo prison and has functioned as a watch tower on the North Gate of the city walls.

The Vikings

By the eleventh century, the Danes (dubbed 'Vikings' by the Saxons, meaning 'pirates') controlled the North and Midlands – the area referred to later as the Danelaw – and had large populations in several towns in the South, including Oxford.

Saxon king Ethelred the Unready (his name meaning 'royal counsel, uncounselled') reasserted English dominance in the south by ordering reprisals against the Danes – who, he said, had 'sprung like weeds among the wheat'. The massacre was planned for St Brice's Day, 13 November 1002. This was the traditional time of year for slaughtering livestock and bull baiting, and Ethelred hoped to catch the mood of bloody necessity.

In Oxford the call to arms was taken up enthusiastically and the local Danes, vastly outnumbered, sought sanctuary in the church of St Frideswide's Priory on the site of modern Christ Church Cathedral. There they were cornered: the Saxons torched the building, with the Danes inside, mopping up with their swords and arrows any Dane who tried to flee.

In an alternative version of the story, Oxford was the venue for a treaty-signing session between Danish generals, Sigeferth and Morkere, and Saxon ealdorman Eadric. The Viking guests were butchered during supper, and it was their avenging army that was cornered and roasted in St Frideswide's.

Whatever the details, this massacre inspired King Sweyn Forkbeard of Denmark, Norway and Sweden to invade

Christ Church Cathedral, where the Danes sought sanctuary.

and add 'England' to his list of dominions a few years later. His sister Gunnhild, one of the hostages handed to Ethelred to seal the temporary peace before the massacre, had been killed – and he wanted revenge. The first reprisals against Oxford came in 1009. A chronicle of the time records that, 'after midwinter the Danes took an excursion up through Chiltern, and so to Oxford; which city they burned, and plundered on both sides of the Thames to their ships'.

In 1013 Sweyn, after several false starts during the previous decade, invaded, and conquered the whole island. Although his reign was brief, his son and grandsons, Cnut, Harold I and Harthacnut, reigned for twenty-six years between them. The kings of England were Anglo-Danes for the next half century.

Edmund II (Ironside) was murdered at Oxford in 1016 after a seven-month reign. His successor Cnut, son of Sweyn, had more success, residing in Oxford where he held many councils between 1016 and 1035. His son Harold I (called Harold Harefoot on account of his great speed on the hunting field) was crowned in Oxford in 1035.

When Harold died in Oxford on 17 March 1040, the citizens praised him for his good timing. His brother Harthacnut was preparing to invade and seize the throne, but Harold's death made the violence unnecessary. The cause of Harold's death is unknown. The Danes said he had been 'elf-struck' (i.e. killed by elves – the origin of the word for the affliction known as a 'stroke'). His brother's death two years later, after some form of seizure, suggests that strokes may have been a genetic condition in the family.

Harold was buried at Westminster Abbey, but his sibling wanted symbolic victory. He had the corpse exhumed and beheaded, and it was dumped in a Thameside bog. Fishermen rescued it after Harthacnut's coronation, and it was buried in the main Danish cemetery in London, and later reburied at St Clement Danes in Westminster.

The Normans

After the Conquest in 1066, vast areas of the country
north of London were trashed in a show of power from
the new Norman overlords. Oxford was levelled in 1067
and much of the land was described as 'waste' in the
aftermath, with 478 houses so ruined that they could
not be assessed for tax purposes. To put this in context,
counting the taxable households inside and outside the
city walls, only 243 were deemed habitable.

Cowed Oxfordshire was up for grabs. Most of it went
to King William's relatives Odo of Bayeaux, Robert
D'Oilly and William FitzOsbern. Odo owned vast
swathes in the Headington, Bampton and Wootton
regions, D'Oilly received Oxford and much more
besides, while FitzOsbern went on to become Earl of
Hereford, Gloucester, Worcester and Oxfordshire, one
of England's richest landowners and castle builders.
During William's absences, FitzOsbern was practically
in charge of the country.

The task of rebuilding Oxford fell to High Sheriff of
Oxford Robert D'Oilly, one of the chief landowners
of the eleventh century post-Norman Conquest. His
legacy can be seen in the surviving St George's Tower at
Oxford Castle. The former church of St Peter-in-the-East
(now part of the university's St Edmund Hall) belonged
to him too, although the oldest surviving sections of the
current building date from 1140. D'Oilly also made the
original 'Oxen ford' into a sturdy bridge, at the point now
known as Folly Bridge on St Aldates.

D'Oilly married Ealdgyth, a Saxon heiress from Wallingford, to consolidate his territorial dominance in the region. As ruthless as any other rich landowner throughout history, Robert once confiscated some meadows just beyond the Oxford city walls, to further his estates. The land had belonged to the monastery at Abingdon, and the aggrieved monks prayed for divine intervention. A few days later Robert had a nightmare in which he was dragged before the Virgin Mary, who made him stand in his pilfered meadows while he was scourged by small boys. So shocked was D'Oilly by this vision that, under his wife's devout guidance, he gave money and land to the monks of Abingdon, and restored all the churches he could find in and around Oxford. Churches which, as historian Andrew Lang pointed out in the 1920s, 'he and his men had helped to ruin'.

Robert D'Oilly's nephew, another Robert, founded Osney Abbey. Only a converted outbuilding remains of this once mighty edifice. The other city-shaping event of the Norman period was the arrival of Beaumont Palace as a royal seat in Oxford. It was built during the reign of Henry I (1100–1135).

The Anarchy

King Stephen was the nephew of outgoing King Henry I. Henry's only legitimate son, William Adelin, had died in a shipwreck in 1120, along with one of Henry's several illegitimate children, Richard. This left the King's legitimate daughter, Matilda, as the direct heir. Stephen, however, seized the throne, leading to a period of brutal civil war known as the Anarchy.

Matilda was not a popular figure, spending hardly any time in England prior to Henry's death. But Stephen was unpopular too, and in 1139 Matilda sailed to England to physically stake her claim to the island, while her husband Geoffrey of Anjou attacked Stephen's Dukedom in Normandy.

After an abortive start to her counter-coup, the Queen gained the upper hand and was crowned Empress Matilda in London. But when the townsfolk rose up against her, she retreated, crown and all, to Oxford, holing up at the heavily fortified castle. Stephen wasted no time in besieging the city. The castle was battered and all looked lost, so Matilda donned a disguise and slipped out of the fortress one freezing winter's night. Wearing white to blend in with the snowy landscape, she crossed the frozen Thames and escaped to the stronghold of Wallingford Castle.

Forces regrouped, and with her son Henry 'Curtmantle' (named after the short robes which he brought to the Anjou fashion scene) at her side, Matilda controlled the south-west of England, while Stephen controlled much of the south-east. There were no more decisive battles, and now the true horrors of the Anarchy descended, a period possibly matched but not exceeded by the very grimmest events in this island's history. The nobles of the land became local tyrants, and the records known to us as the Anglo-Saxon Chronicle comment that Stephen's nineteen-year reign was a time when 'Christ and his Saints slept'.

Stephen was eventually forced into a peace treaty that bypassed his son Eustace in favour of Matilda's boy Henry (II). Stephen died in 1154, and Henry, often residing at Beaumont Palace in Oxford, reigned until 1189.

The Plantagenets

King Henry II (1133–89) kick-started Oxford's growth after the darkness of the previous 300 years. He granted the city a royal charter and encouraged rudimentary economic and academic development through privileges and incentives. Religious houses flourished. The friar-scholars who settled as teachers during the twelfth century were probably carrying on an established proto-university tradition, but the historical record is vague. Chronicles mention Master Robert Puleyn as a lecturer in divinity in 1133, clearly a part of an established centre of learning. With St Frideswyde's Priory and Osney Abbey fully functioning, this is not altogether surprising.

Parliaments were regularly held from Beaumont Palace (at a site near modern Beaumont Street, birthplace of Kings Richard I and John). The Provisions of Oxford were drawn up here in the reign of Henry III (1207–72) by Earl of Leicester Simon de Montfort and his fellow rebellious Barons. The Provisions put their rights and powers on a firm legal footing, and have been described as England's first written constitution. The new deal introduced a powerful council of twenty-four nobles – half selected by the King, half by the Barons. This was the first elected chamber in Europe, and Parliament met thrice yearly to oversee the work of the council.

In 1239 the temporary closure of the University of Paris caused Franciscan scholar-friars to emigrate to Oxford. Their *studium* was established on land behind St Ebbe's church. It was here that leading theologian, philosopher and prime mover of the early university John Duns Scotus (1266–1308) received his formative education.

The concept of students accessing university education via a college was founded by Walter de Merton, Chancellor of England. This collegiate system began with the foundation of Merton in 1265, as a community of students bound together by residence, rules, traditions, chapel, refectory and, a little later, the 'quad'.

The university was exempt from the laws that applied to laymen: the origin of the famous 'Town versus Gown' divide. Students were originally clerics, with tonsures (the shaven heads associated with monks) and answered to religious courts – and, ultimately, the Papacy.

The rise of the hall and, later, college system was an attempt to maintain the clerical/secular divide. Students originally lodged with townsfolk as 'chamberdekyns', and soon succumbed to the secular habits (i.e. wine, women and song) of the ordinary citizen. Herded into halls, under a Master or Principal, the intention was to spare them the many temptations of the Oxford streets. The apartheid lasted into the nineteenth century, with annual 'Town versus Gown' head-to-heads.

The linking of a college with a particular source of students was established in the reign of Richard II by William of Wykeham, founder of New College in 1379. His college was linked with Winchester School. Since then, colleges have often been associated with towns or regions.

After an infamous 'Town versus Gown' riot in 1355, the university was given over-arching powers to rule the city. This shaped the daggers-drawn relationship of townsmen and university men for the next 500 years.

King Henry IV (1366–1413) frequently set up court at Beaumont Palace, and his son Henry V (1386–1422) was a student at Queen's College. The latter is also associated with All Souls (founded 1438). The marriage of Henry V to Katherine of France was in the minds of Queens' founders when they made their dedication.

The High Street gateway of All Souls is decorated with carved souls. The college was founded not just as a place of learning but as a chantry, a place of prayer endowed with money to act as a permanent memorial to the dead. Warden and fellows of the college were instructed to pray for the souls of everyone – a pretty stiff challenge – in particular 'the illustrious Prince Henry [V], late King of England, Thomas, Duke of Clarence, and of all the Dukes, Earls, Barons, Knights, Esquires, and others who fell in the war for the Crown of France'.

Edward IV (1442–70) preferred the palace at Langley in Oxfordshire, with its access to the royal hunting grounds of Wychwood Forest. But he was a great supporter of academia, and assumed the title Protector of the University of Oxford. He visited the newly completed Magdalen College on 22 September 1481, entering the city by torchlight where he was welcomed by the university's Chancellor (also the King's brother-in-law), Lionel Woodville.

This began a short-lived royal patronage of Magdalen. In 1483 Edward's brother and successor Richard III stayed at the college and listened to debates in the college hall. He was impressed enough to reward the institution with money and venison. The man who toppled Richard, Henry VII, stayed here too and a requiem Mass is still sung for him each year at the college. His eldest son Arthur (the doomed elder brother of Henry VIII) lodged at Magdalen three times, and the college president Richard Mayhew was one of the deputation sent to Spain to collect Prince Arthur's bride-to-be (and Henry's, as it happened), Katherine of Aragon.

The Tudors

An epidemic known as the sweating sickness, or English sweat, ravaged Oxford in 1517, halving the population of the city (and Cambridge too). The outbreak is thought to have been linked to appalling hygiene conditions and/or a lice-borne virus.

Henry VIII permanently changed the landscape of Oxford, closing down its various religious houses and establishing his own King Henry VIII's college (now known as Christ Church). Meanwhile, the colleges' refusal to abandon Catholicism caused tensions and outbreaks of violence that were to colour the reigns of Henry and his three successors.

The most famous victims of these turbulent times were the 'Oxford Martyrs' – bishops Hugh Latimer and Nicholas Ridley, and Archbishop Thomas Cranmer. In October 1555, Catholic Queen 'Bloody' Mary I, in a violent attempt to remedy the Protestant lurch, condemned these three men to burn at the stake in the town ditch (now Broad Street). The alleged spot is marked with a cross on the road.

Latimer and Ridley went to the flames first, Ridley telling his friend that God would either lessen the pain of the flames, or bolster their spirits to withstand it. In turn, Latimer consoled his companion at the bonfire: 'Be of good cheer, Ridley, and play the man. We shall this day, by God's grace, light up such a candle in England as I trust will never be put out.'

Cranmer followed them to the flames in March the following year. He had recanted, out of fear for his life, but facing the flames he now declared, 'This is the hand that wrote it [the recantation], and therefore shall it suffer first punishment.' As the fire mounted, Cranmer allowed his right hand to burn. Sources say he cried out, 'This hand hath offended!' or, 'This unworthy right hand!' throughout.

When Elizabeth I ascended the throne, it was the Catholics' turn to suffer. In 1589 priests George Nichols, Richard Yaxley, Thomas Belson and Humphrey Pritchard were executed in Oxford at a site on Holywell Street (marked with a plaque).

Elizabeth was the first monarch to receive a monetary gift from the university when she visited in 1566. She was presented with a silver cup worth £10, containing £40 in gold (combined value of about £6,000 in today's money). Prior to this visit, monarchs had been given traditional gifts such as oxen, sheep, lambs, veal calves and loaves of sugar.

Elizabeth visited Oxford to impress on the townsfolk her resolute views, particularly in matters of religious inclinations. She was here to mark the city as Anglican Protestant, and purge Catholicism and the equally troublesome Puritanism. In a speech at the university, she said: 'I mean to let the scholars see that I am not in the humour to stand any nonsense.'

Stuarts and Civil War

The accession of King James I was marked by plague. It started in London in 1603 and spread to Oxford. Most students fled, and the Michaelmas term had to be cancelled. All college gates were kept shut, shops were closed – even cats and dogs vanished from the streets. Grass is said to have grown in the thoroughfares.

James' son Charles I famously chose the city as his base in 1643 during the Civil War. The university was predominantly pro-Royalist, making Oxford a natural choice. His Court and Parliament installed itself at Christ Church, while his Queen's retinue requisitioned Merton. Their sons, Charles and James, and nephews Prince Rupert and Prince Maurice, installed their own enormous households too, with the symbolic assent of pro-Royalist University Chancellor Archbishop Laud (who had been imprisoned in the Tower of London by Parliament).

New College was transformed into a warehouse of munitions and hardware, while Oriel produced cannons and housed the King's Privy Council. The Mill at Osney set to work grinding gunpowder instead of flour. New Inn hall became the Oxford Mint, churning out coinage to pay the army, using melted down college plate and other metalware purloined from university and household alike. The new university schools at the Bodleian became stores for foodstuffs and workshops for clothing and other necessities.

The inhabitants of Oxford were heavily taxed to finance the King's military takeover. All men aged between sixteen and forty-five were forced to enlist in the army, a gibbet was erected at Carfax and the plague that continued to rage through the populace simply added insult to injury.

The Parliamentarians began the first of three sieges of the city in June 1644, and the king decided to leave town before the fighting began in earnest. While a chunk of his army heaved towards Abingdon as a diversion, Charles briefed his Privy Council on general tactics and fled the city disguised as his sons' tutor's servant, at 9 p.m. on 3 June.

At the beginning of 1645, Oliver Cromwell's New Model Army declared the seizure of Oxford its number one priority, and on 21 May the Parliamentarians' military mastermind Thomas Fairfax began the siege. He watched proceedings from the frontline, literally dodging bullets on one occasion, while his artillery proved how far it could penetrate the enemy ranks when a cannon ball was fired from Old Marston to the walls of Christ Church 1 mile away. But the killer blow proved elusive, and in November that year Charles was able to take up residence in Oxford once again. Fairfax installed himself at 17 Mill Lane, Marston, now known as 'Cromwell House', scene of negotiations over the long-drawn out Treaty of Oxford a few months later.

Charles managed to flee Oxford yet again in April 1646. Skirmishes continued, even while a peace treaty was being hammered out. When, on 20 June 1646, the Royalists officially surrendered, Charles' commanders felt betrayed by the politicians and the king, claiming they could still win the battle for Oxford. But it was all bluster. The treaty was signed at the Audit House, Christ Church, by the Governor of Oxford and Thomas Fairfax.

On 22 June the fallen hero Prince Rupert and 300 Royalist aristocrats were given safe passage from the city, and two days later the Treaty came into operation. Fairfax's army patrolled the streets to maintain order, and the Royalist evacuation began. The 3,000 soldiers, who had survived three successive sieges, were marched from the city. Charles went to the block on 30 January 1649.

The Later Stuarts

The Civil War hostilities, seemingly exhausted, weren't actually over at all. The Parliamentarians encountered a lot of negative feedback from Royalist Oxford. Mrs Fell, the wife of the Dean of Christ Church, refused to vacate the premises when requested to do so, and she had to be carried bodily into the quadrangle, screaming abuse at her man-handlers, a squad of Cromwell's musketeers.

During the Commonwealth of Oliver and Richard Cromwell (1649–60), Oxford picked up the pieces and thrived, with most of the colleges having heads elected by the post-monarchy establishment. Both Cromwells were Chancellor of the university during their years in power, but college heads installed under the Commonwealth were unceremoniously booted out in the Restoration after Charles II ascended in 1660. In many cases, this was little more than a spiteful political gesture, and bad news for academia. Historian Anthony Wood was one of the era's witnesses. 'Some Cavaliers that were restored were good scholars, but the majority were dunces,' he commented. One of the worst struck was Exeter College, which received Joseph Maynard as its head, or Rector:

> Exeter College is now much debauched by a drunken Governor whereas, before, in Doctor Conant's time, it was accounted a civil house, it is now rude and uncivil... The Rector is good-natured, generous and a good scholar, but... he is much given to bibbing [drinking], and... he will sit there, smoke, and drink till he is drunk, and has to be led to his lodgings.

Wood was equally scathing when assessing the new breed of Restoration student: 'Their aim is not to live as students ought to do,' he said, 'but to live like gentry, to keep dogs and horses, to turn their studies into places to keep bottles, to swagger in gay apparel and long periwigs.'

Charles II set up court in Oxford during the Great Plague of London, 1665–66. His successor James II caused a minor uprising when he installed a Catholic head at Magdalen College in 1687. In spite of this unpopular interference, Oxford retained Jacobite (i.e. pro-Stuart, supporting the surviving heirs of the old dynasty) sympathies after the demise of the last Stuart monarch, Queen Anne, in 1714.

When King William III (husband of penultimate Stuart monarch Mary II) visited Oxford in 1695, the Sheldonian Theatre prepared a grand feast. The monarch, however, believed that Jacobite plotters were attempting to poison him and boycotted the party.

The Georgians and Jacobites

When the official celebrations for Hanoverian George I's birthday were enforced in Oxford on 28 May 1715, its Jacobite sympathies manifested in riots, led by university students. A mob dismantled the town's celebratory Georgian bonfire, and any window sporting a candle – a mark of loyal celebration of the King's birthday – was smashed. Presbyterian minister William Roby, staunch supporter of the Hanoverian succession, was put in the town stocks, and his effigy was burnt. There were too few town constables to disperse the crowds.

Pro-Stuart feeling peaked on the following day, the anniversary of the Restoration of King Charles II. People ran through the streets shouting, 'King James III! The true king! No usurper!' Oriel, a pro-Hanoverian College, was stoned and several people were injured.

The city lacked the will to join the organised national anti-George revolt, however, and the clergy's official line was to condemn the Jacobites. In spite of strong support for the uprising in 1715, and an unofficial stocktaking of the available men, horses and arms who could support the rebel Duke of Ormond (who was expected to lead the Jacobite cause in the south), order was maintained. The Mayor spoke of 'pestilent fellows who fomented sedition' even as open chants supporting 'James III' and Ormond were heard from gangs promenading the streets. Three chief Oxford conspirators, Gordon, Kerr and Dorwell, were sentenced to death and hanged at Tyburn in London on 7 December 1715.

The 1745 rebellion of 'Young Pretender' Charles Edward Stuart, grandson of James II, made it as far south as Derby before retreating and meeting its nemesis at the Battle of Culloden the following year. But there were still many citizens in England who wanted to remove the incumbent Hanoverian Georges from the throne, and Oxford folklore maintains that two Jacobite students were hanged under Magdalen Bridge in 1745 for belonging to the pro-Pretender White Rose Club.

In February 1748 anti-Hanoverians took to the streets again. The university's Vice Chancellor, Proctors and Heads feared that things were careering towards revolution, and in April they formally condemned the students involved, making 'a public declaration of our sincere abhorrence and detestation of such factions and seditious practices, as also of our firm resolution to punish offenders (of what state or quality soever they are) who shall duly be convicted thereof, according to the uttermost severity and rigour of our statutes.'

The 'soever they are' note warned offenders that they would not be able to hide behind titles and peerages. Several ringleaders – 'beardless striplings of sedition' according to the summary in *The Newgate Calendar*, one of the most popular collections of the nineteenth century – were arrested.

Much of Oxford retains a 'Georgian' flavour in architectural terms. Many older buildings now sport eighteenth-century façades; and new icons, such as the Clarendon building and Holywell Music Rooms, were erected in this period. The frontage of Queen's College is a monument to the era, with its statue of George II's Queen, Caroline, decorating the roof in a stone cupola.

The Victorians

Although Oxford has medieval college foundations and Georgian façades, many of the larger landmark buildings were built in the nineteenth century. Examples include the Ashmolean, the Natural History/Pitt Rivers complex, the Town Hall, the Randolph Hotel, the Oxford University Press on Walton Street, the Taylor Institution, the Examination Schools, colleges such as Keble, Hertford, Mansfield, Somerville, St Hugh's, St Hilda's and Lady Margaret Hall. The neo-Gothic design that dominates churches throughout the island, from renovations like St Mary Magdalen on Magdalen Street to new builds such as St Frideswide's on Botley Road and St Ebbe's behind the Westgate shopping centre, is also nineteenth-century.

The great liberation of the navel-gazing, ineffectual and impractical university began with the University Act of 1854, which made it possible for non-Church of England members to study at Oxford. By the 1870s a new mental climate had swept in, side-lining the denominational tussles, and (after 1875) generating waves of female students and academics – still in their own segregated schools and colleges, but able for the first time to take advantage of Oxford University resources.

The university now adopted the continental model of offering BA degrees based on separate schools (history, mathematics, literature, natural sciences, medicine, etc.) and shifted from the farcical five-minute oral examination to gruelling written exams, taken in the newly built Examination Schools.

Victorian Oxford in all of its splendour.

The Great Western Railway, which had opened its station near Folly Bridge in 1814, linked Oxford to London in 1837. With the arrival of other rail lines the long reign (and reins) of the horse-drawn coach was finally at an end. A proposal in 1865 to establish the Great Western's workshops at Oxford was fended off by the still-powerful college dons who thought it would spoil the character of the city, taking no account of the men it would employ and the thousands it would benefit.

Away from the university, the bulk of the population remained poor and there were many slum areas, notably St Ebbe's, St Thomas' and St Clements. These were the centres of three major outbreaks of cholera in 1832, 1849, and 1854. Oxford was also affected by the national waves of protest and riot that coloured the century.

Revolutionary change was felt elsewhere in the city, with the final triumph of Town over Gown. The university had run the city since the St Scholastica's Day riot in 1355.

A Brief History of Oxford

In 1771 the city and the university began to run Oxford together, but it was the 1836 Municipal Corporation Act that paved the way for fundamental change, including a rudimentary city police force, and a Local Board of Health (established in 1865 and jointly populated by Town and Gown). This supervised such areas as paving, lighting, hygiene, flood control, fire brigade, tramways and general improvements. Finally, in 1889, the city corporation took on these roles itself. Oxford became a county borough, and the modern city was upon us.

Twentieth Century

In the early twentieth century Oxford experienced the industrial and population growth typical of much of the country. The biggest increase came with the establishment of Morris Motors Limited and the associated Pressed Steel Company in Cowley, both spearheaded by William Morris (later Lord Nuffield and founder of Nuffield College). Between them these companies employed thousands of Oxfordians. In its modern guise as BMW's Mini plant (known as Plant Oxford and complemented by Plant Swindon a few miles to the west), the car business is still an important part of the city's economy. Oxford Business Park occupies a large section of the former Morris plant.

During the two world wars the university colleges became temporary military barracks, training grounds and hospitals. Oxford avoided damage in both wars, lacking the heavy industry or strategic targets that first the Zeppelins and then the Blitz sought. Hitler also planned to establish his English HQ in Oxford after the war, so had no intention of flattening it.

Women who had been studying in Oxford for forty-five years were finally allowed to take Oxford University degrees in 1920. The rise of the institution currently known as Oxford Brookes University brought an even greater influx of students to the city. The institution has reinvented itself constantly through the decades, and is currently undergoing a massive rebuild.

The last of the city's slums were cleared in the 1950s. Compulsory daily worship was abandoned by the university early in the century, the requirement to have a working knowledge of Ancient Greek was removed in 1920 and in 1960 it was decided that Latin, the linguistic foundation of the western academic world, was no longer a prerequisite.

For all its superficially antique air, Oxford and its surrounding county had the highest growth rate of 'high-tech' information technology and science-based businesses in the UK during the century, the bulk of them tracing their roots back to the university. The trend continues today: Oxford Science Park plays host to nearly seventy digitally enhanced companies, and businesses such as technology transfer company Isis Innovation in Summertown give a fair indication of the thoroughly modern stuff that rushed in to fill the void left by daily worship, Ancient Greek and Latin.

Chapter Two

Oxford
Colleges

There are forty-four colleges and permanent private halls in the University of Oxford. The 'collegiate' system allows students and academics to be part of the larger university whilst rooted in the rich vat of history, tradition and eccentricity of an Oxford college, with all their associated sense of identity and extra-curricular opportunities. Every college and hall in the collegiate system is independent, but works within a framework set by the university, teaching standard university-approved courses.

The much-celebrated separateness of the colleges is a bit of an illusion, however. They all cooperate, and students study according to their subject rather than their college. The academic structure is what truly defines the university. It is based on subject-specific departments: the institution should be viewed as a federation of departments rather than a gentleman's club of colleges.

The institution has not enjoyed uninterrupted academic progression and excellence. The fifteenth-century Wars of the Roses drained the young men from the country. The chaos of war was compounded by the ravages of plague and, by the time Henry VII brought matters to a close at the Battle of Bosworth in 1485, there wasn't much of the functioning university left.

Other declines and decimations were less excusable. In the 1530s the commissioners of the Reformation's royally-sanctioned thug Thomas Cromwell reported gleefully that the library at New College had been trashed. The books, of Catholic origin, were deemed 'superstitious' and therefore evil and worthless. Many were associated with one of the thirteenth century's leading academics John Duns Scotus, referred to by Commissioner Layton as 'Dunce'. They were ripped apart and thrown into the college quad. Layton reported:

We have set Dunce in Bocardo [the city gaol], and utterly banished him from Oxford forever, with all his blind glosses... And the second time we came to New College we found all the great quadrant full of leaves of Dunce, the wind blowing them into every corner. And there we found a certain Mr Greenfield, a gentleman of Buckinghamshire, gathering up part of the said book leaves, as he said, therewith to make him sewells or blanchers, to keep the deer within the wood, thereby to have the better cry with his hounds. [Sewells and blanchers are old words for scarecrow-like items placed in a wood to prevent deer from accessing certain paths or areas. Greenfield's ill-gotten harvest of 'leaves' would have been parchment.]

The vandalism continued across the university. Many manuscripts were piled onto bonfires, 'guilty of no other superstition than red letters in the front of titles' said one nineteenth-century historian. Anything depicting angels was destroyed, as these were now viewed as diabolical, Catholic, or both. From Merton College alone, a full cartload of manuscripts was removed. A Dutch man called Herks rescued some and wisely stored them in the Bodleian Library.

Site of the Bocardo, 1770.

The librarian at Balliol, a man called Persons, sold most of the college's old books in order to purchase Protestant ones. Some collections were sold for waste paper at the price of twenty pieces of silver per library (or forty shillings). This is either a desecration of antiquities, or a pragmatic stock issue familiar to any cash-strapped librarian, depending on which way you look at it.

By the time Edward VI (1537–53) was on the throne, most librarians were out of work. Books were associated with worldliness and idolatry, which served to undermine the whole principle of libraries in Oxford. As nineteenth-century historian Andrew Lang wrote:

Oxford was almost empty. The schools were used by laundresses as a place wherein clothes might conveniently be dried. The citizens encroached on academic property. Some schools were quite destroyed, and the sites converted into gardens. The college plate and jewels left by pious benefactors were stolen, and went to the melting pot. Thus flourished Oxford under Edward VI.

It is easy to pass judgement on these actions, especially the more visually obvious vandalism of destroyed monasteries and brutally defaced church monuments and ornaments. But, perched in our secular twenty-first-century ivory towers, it is almost impossible to imagine the passions involved. The Reformation wasn't the Conservatives versus Labour: it was two world-views colliding.

Things were equally grim in the Puritan era of the seventeenth century and the university's alarming academic decline did not end here. In the Georgian era the college experience was little more than a rite (and right) of passage for rich young men. In the early nineteenth century an Oxford degree was to be obtained by a simple interview with a tutor at the end of the allotted period. Men received honours degrees after answering two questions: 'What is the meaning of "Golgotha"?' and 'Who founded University College?' That the 'correct' answer to the second question was 'King Alfred', and that this 'fact' was founded on legend rather than historical verity, turns the farce into something even more farcical.

King Alfred.

After centuries of decline the university began to get its act together in the later nineteenth century. During the twentieth it rose again to become a pre-eminent academic institution. Implicitly conservative, change has always been slow, but recent reorganisations and streamlining have equipped it for a highly successful life in the twenty-first century, without losing too much of its essentially eccentric, chaotic charm.

And much of that charm lies in the idiosyncrasies of the university's thirty-eight private colleges and six permanent private halls…

All Souls College, High Street

Alternative names: The College of All Souls of the Faithful Departed of Oxford. Its official corporate designation is The Warden and the College of the Souls of all Faithful People Deceased in the University of Oxford. It is named after the church calendar feast of All Souls, 2 November.

Founders: Seventeen-year-old Henry VI and Archbishop of Canterbury Robert Chichele, 1438.

College secrets: The imposing twin towers were designed by Nicholas Hawksmoor, and the Back Quad (visible from Radcliffe Square) has a sundial designed by Christopher Wren. Its dial has a Latin inscription translating as: 'The hours pass away and are counted against us.' Prior to our current digital age, it is said to have set the time for all the clock and watch-makers of the university.

The college 'Mallard Song' stems from a unique All Souls' tradition, Hunting the Mallard. Originally an annual drunken romp through, and over, the college buildings, in the seventeenth century the celebration was limited to once a century, for reasons of rowdyism. The Hunt duly occurred in 1701, 1801, 1901 and 2001, but readers of this book will be long in the beak before

All Souls College, High Street.

the next bout in 2101. Folklore claims that the custom originated with a giant duck, which was flushed from the building's foundations.

There are no undergraduates, and the college is a registered charity. All Souls has several non-academic fellows who bridge the college's academic and public personas, working in areas such as law, economics, politics and international relations. This odd academic/public relationship was created by Sir William Anson, College Warden 1881–1914. Such was his impact that he was dubbed 'second founder' of the college.

Famous alumni and fellows: Fifteenth-century physician and humanist Thomas Linacre; seventeenth-century University Chancellor and Archbishop of Canterbury Gilbert Sheldon; architect Christopher Wren; philosopher Sir Isaiah Berlin; historians A.L. Rowse, Rosemary Hill; economist Amartya Sen; politician Quintin Hogg, Baron Hailsham of St Marylebone; MPs John Redwood, William Waldegrave.

Balliol College, Broad Street

Alternative name: The Master and Scholars of Balliol College.

Founders: John I de Balliol and his wife Dervorguilla, Scottish aristocrats, around 1263.

College secrets: Greek Orthodox Church ambassador Nathanael Konopios introduced coffee-drinking to England during his visit to Balliol in the 1630s.

In 1642 King Charles I, holed up in Oxford during the Civil War, demanded of Balliol all its ready cash and silver plate. The loan was never repaid, and no formal offer of repayment has ever been made. Subsequently money became a major problem for Balliol, and when it lost many of its rents through the Great Fire of London in 1666, it was on the verge of closure.

In 1973 Balliol became the first of the all-male Oxford colleges to elect a woman as a fellow and tutor. Women were finally admitted as students in 1979.

In 1452 George Neville, brother of 'Warwick the King Maker', hosted a feast at Balliol College. It was claimed to be the largest supper ever served in the city. On the first day he served three courses consisting of 600 platters of meat. The second course alone featured beef, venison, 'carcell', partridge, crane, peacock, rabbit, curlew, plus fritters and 'a subtlety'. No veg, note. 'Subtleties' were elaborate table decorations made of sugar, paste, jelly or wax, usually a locally relevant sculpture of buildings, ships, animals and suchlike. They were also known as 'warners', warning diners that the meat fest was about to commence.

Famous alumni and fellows: Fourteenth-century bible translator John Wycliffe; father of modern capitalism Adam Smith; welfare state architect William Beveridge; Prime Ministers Herbert Asquith, Harold Macmillan and Edward Heath; kings Olav V and Harald V of Norway, and Yang di-Pertuan Besar of Malaysia; poets Robert Southey, Matthew Arnold, Gerard Manley Hopkins; writers Hilaire Belloc, Aldous Huxley, Graham Greene, Christopher Hitchens; diarist John Evelyn; Nobel-prize winning scientists Oliver Smithies, C.N. Hinshelwood and Anthony Leggett; current household names Richard Dawkins, Peter and Dan Snow, Boris Johnson, Yvette Cooper and Amit Chaudhuri.

Blackfriars Hall, St Giles

Alternative names: Blackfriars Priory, Latin *Aula Fratrum Praedicatorum* (Hall of the Brothers of the Order of Preachers).

Founder: Father Bede Jarrett, 15 August 1921. He was the first Dominican friar to study at Oxford since the sixteenth-century Reformation.

College secrets: This is the third Priory foundation by Black Friars in Oxford. The first was in 1221, the second (having outgrown Priory number one) in 1245.

The institution harks back to the true origins of the university as a community of academic friars. Blackfriars houses twenty-odd Dominicans, staying true to the medieval timetable of communal prayer, study, and preaching. The chief subjects are theology and philosophy, with just a smattering of literature, classics and history. The friars belong to the Order of Preachers, which is an international religious order in the Catholic Church, and Oxford is the Studium (study house) of the Order in England. Black Friars' architect was Doran Webb; but construction of the site stopped in 1929 when funds ran short. The community moved in during that year, but the building is still unfinished. It became part of the university collegiate system in 1994.

Founder of the order Saint Dominic (1170–1221) was born in Caleruega, Spain, where he is known as Domingo Félix de Guzmán. He founded his Ordo Praedicatorum (Order of Preachers) in 1216.

Famous alumni and fellows: Dr James Alison, British Theologian; Delia Gallagher, CNN Faith and Values Correspondent; Brian Davies, Philosopher; Anthony Fisher, Catholic Bishop of Parramatta, Australia; Timothy Radcliffe, Past Master of the Order of Preachers (clerical).

Brasenose College, Radcliffe Square

Alternative names: The King's Hall and College of Brasenose.

Founders: Sir Richard Sutton, lawyer, and William Smyth, Bishop of Lincoln, 1512. They were both from the north-west of England, and Brasenose has always maintained links with Lancashire and Cheshire. The college replaced the far earlier Brasenose Hall.

College secrets: The name Brasenose almost certainly derives from the 'brazen' (brass or bronze) door knocker, whose nose clearly captured students' imagination when the college was founded in the thirteenth century. The only alternative theory in with a chance is one that claims the name means *brasen huis*, an old term for a brewhouse. Brasenose was, indeed, famous for its beer.

View in Radcliffe Square.

The college's first bursar, Roland Messenger, was *persona non grata*, for reasons that have slipped through the sieve of history. New Brasenose fellows had to swear 'not to admit him to the college for more than one day.' So dire was the warning that the oath was still being taken more than 300 years after Messenger had died.

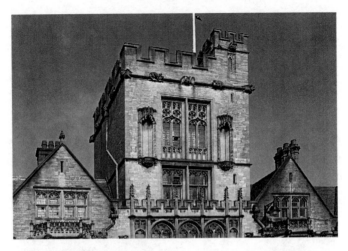

Brasenose Tower, High Street. (Photograph by Jan Sullivan)

During the Civil War, Charles I turned Brasenose into a camp for the Royalist army, and academic work pretty much ground to a halt. At the time, the college had been in bad debt; but after the war it managed to reverse its fortunes, becoming ostentatiously wealthy. This was not all good, attracting the kind of aristocratic student who preferred to spend the day hunting and patronising horse racetracks.

The bugles in the college coat of arms echo these hunting horns of old. They are part of founder Richard Sutton's insignia; the benefactor can be seen in a very striking portrait in the college hall, dressed in a literal coat of arms – a garment decorated with the insignia, bugles and all. Another interesting feature of the coat of arms is a golden Virgin Mary, holding Jesus and a sceptre, and seated on a tombstone (one of the symbols of the Diocese of Lincoln, to which Oxford belonged when the college was founded: the Diocese of Oxford was not created until 1542).

Famous alumni and fellows: Elias Ashmole, founder of the Ashmolean Museum; writers John *Richard Hannay* Buchan, William *Lord of the Flies* Golding and poet Thomas Traherne; Colin Cowdrey, cricketer; Arthur Evans, the archaeologist associated with the palace of Minos on Crete; Stanley Hooker, Rolls Royce engine designer; John Gorton, Australian Prime Minister; Robert Runcie, Archbishop of Canterbury; Michael Palin, comedian, Python, TV tour guide.

Campion Hall, Brewer Street

Founder: The Society of Jesus (the Jesuits), 1896. They own and run the building, and named it after sixteenth-century Catholic martyr Thomas Campion.

College secrets: A permanent private hall rather than a college, Campion nevertheless enjoys the same status as the colleges in the university structure. Campion was designed to house ordained priests – as it says on the college's perfunctory website: 'Please note that laymen are only admitted occasionally and for special reasons'.

In 2013 the community consisted of thirty-five men, two thirds of whom were Jesuits. The Jesuits are a Roman Catholic male religious order, founded in 1539 by Ignatius of Loyola. The founder had a military background, and preached a message of obedience and conformity which led to the Jesuits' nickname God's Marines – a gung-ho approach that has had its downsides, to put it mildly, in certain areas of their missionary work. It is far better to dwell on their commitment to education and social justice in the modern world – a worthy battle indeed.

Famous alumni and fellows: Count Michael Anthony Maurice de la Bédoyère, author and journalist; Fr Martin Cyril D'Arcy, priest and philosopher; John Maurice Florescu, political adviser, chief executive officer of

Centrade (Houston); Peter John L'Estrange, Australian Jesuit priest and historian; Peter Chad Tigar Levi, writer, reviewer, archaeologist; Cardinal George Pell, Archbishop of Sydney.

Christ Church College, St Aldates

Alternative names: The Dean, Chapter and Students of the Cathedral Church of Christ in Oxford of the Foundation of King Henry the Eighth (or the snappier *Aedes Christi* in Latin). It was called King Henry VIII's College 1529–34, and before this it was Cardinal's College (1524–29), founded by Henry's soon-to-fall-from-favour right-hand man Cardinal Thomas Wolsey.

Founder: King Henry VIII, serial wife-seeker and despot, in 1524. Refounded 1546.

College secrets: This college probably steals more chapter space in books about Oxford than any other due to its illustrious alumni and all-round eccentricity. It is unique in being a joint college and cathedral institution. The head of the college is a Church of England Dean and its college chapel doubles as Oxford's Cathedral, HQ of the Diocese of Oxford. Christ Church also has a world-famous Cathedral Choir, an art gallery of national importance and more treasure than you could shake a pirate at.

Wolsey created his college from the twelfth-century St Frideswide's Priory, and the old church remains at the centre of the modern college. The Priory was dissolved, not by Henry VIII, but by a papal bull (a decree from the Pope) granted to Wolsey.

Choir directors (known as Organists, whether they play the instrument or not) have included such famous names as John Taverner (installed by Wolsey) and William Walton. Their recorded work has ranged from sacred texts to the theme music for *Mr Bean* and *The Vicar of Dibley*.

Pembroke College Chapel and Tom Tower.

After the Restoration in 1660 the college was rewarded for its loyalty to Charles I during the Civil War. The reward financed the completion of Tom Quad, named after Great Tom, a bell located in the iconic Tom Tower (designed by Christopher Wren). The bell was a survivor from St Frideswide's Priory, the current version being cast in 1680. Great Tom rings 101 times at five past nine every evening. This represents the original 100 college fellows, plus an extra one added in 1663. The timing reflects Oxford Time, which was five minutes later than standard British time.

The college coat of arms is actually Thomas Wolsey's coat of arms. It features a mish-mash of references, including the Tudor Rose, St Thomas Beckett's symbol of the Cornish chough (a type of crow), the blue leopards of the Dukes of Suffolk (Wolsey's home county) and the red lion of Pope Leo X, who made Wolsey a Cardinal. Wolsey's hat (an optional extra on the coat of arms) survives in a Victorian glass case in the college's Upper Library.

A portrait of Wolsey hangs in the hall (along with one of his nemesis Henry VIII). The Cardinal was always painted in profile as he had a drooping eyelid and did not want it immortalised in paint. It is said that Henry liked to be painted head-on to hide his large ears.

Famous alumni and fellows: Philosopher John Locke; religious leader John Wesley; many famous writers including Richard Hakluyt, W.H. Auden, Lewis Carroll, Jan Morris and Richard Curtis; Albert Einstein (briefly in the 1930s); 13 Prime Ministers including William Gladstone and Anthony Eden; Scientist Robert Hooke; King Edward VII; American Founding Father William 'Pennsylvania' Penn; composers John Dowland, William Walton, Howard Goodall, Michael Flanders and Donald Swann; TV presenters Ludovic Kennedy, David Dimbleby.

Corpus Christi College, Merton Street

Alternative names: The President and Scholars of the College of Corpus Christi in the University of Oxford.

Founder: Richard Foxe, Bishop of Winchester, political adviser to King Henry VII, 1517.

College secrets: The strange bird that haunts Corpus Christi in various frescoes and artworks, and in gaudy gold at the top of the sundial pillar in the Main Quad (completed in 1581 by Charles Turnbull), is a pelican. It doesn't always look like one, as some of the artists and carvers had never seen a specimen, but pelican it is nonetheless. The bird is pecking at its own breast, drawing blood with which to feed its young. In Christian iconography this represents Christ shedding his blood, via death, for mankind; hence the name of the college, meaning 'body of Christ'.

Reginald Pole, fellow of Corpus Christi and Archbishop of Canterbury under Queen Mary I in the mid-sixteenth century, was a candidate for the papacy. He came close to scooping the best seat in the Vatican, but not close enough.

In the nineteenth century, Corpus began to recruit students in open competition, a system familiar to all would-be scholars these days, but quite novel back then.

Corpus Christi pelicans on Merton Street. (Photograph by Jan Sullivan)

Erasmus, the greatest scholar of the early sixteenth century, declared that Corpus's library was *inter praecipua decora Britanniae* – 'among the chief beauties of Britain'.

Corpus's treasures include the original silver plate and Bishop's crozier of its founder Foxe.

Famous alumni and fellows: Seventeenth-century scholar Richard Hooker; MP and founder of Georgia, USA, James Oglethorpe; Anglo-Catholic revival champion and founder of Keble College John Keble; Poet Laureate Robert Bridges; art historian John Ruskin; twentieth-century philosophers Isaiah Berlin and Thomas Nagel; writer Vikram Seth; Labour Party movers and shakers David and Ed Miliband.

Exeter College, Turl Street

Alternative names: The Rector and Scholars of Exeter College in the University of Oxford. The foundation was originally named Stapeldon Hall.

Founder: Walter de Stapeldon, Bishop of Exeter and Treasurer of England under Edward II, 1314.

College secrets: The 'Exeter' tag reflects the founder's home county of Devon. For many centuries the bulk of the college's undergraduates came from Devon and Cornwall. Belying these southern pretensions, the college is also renowned for its traditional Burns Night feast.

Exeter suffered many years of poverty, with little or no money for buildings or inmates. Between 1440 and 1470 the college's biggest outlay was on the construction of a new toilet, costing £4 12*s*.

All that remains of the original, medieval college is Palmer's Tower, built in 1432 and named after a contemporary Rector. The current college complex, still centred on the original site, was laid out between 1618 and 1710, in a new era of prosperity. The 250 previous years of poverty had been brought to an end with a large influx of funding from Exeter alumnus Sir William Petre in 1566. Petre was a talented and wily Tudor politician, functioning profitably through the reigns of Henry VIII, Edward VI, Mary I and Elizabeth I, surfing across the associated social and religious upheavals.

Amongst the college's treasures is the Bohun Psalter, a fourteenth-century illuminated manuscript made for Humphrey de Bohun (1342–73), Earl of Hereford. It was given to William Petre by Queen Elizabeth from her private collection and bears the signatures of Elizabeth of York (wife of Henry VII, Elizabeth's grandfather) and Katherine of Aragon (Henry VIII's first wife, mother of Catholic Mary I).

The origins of Oxford's love affair with boat clubs and races begins at Exeter. The Exeter boat first appeared in 1824, and the college's boat club records are the university's earliest, dating from 1831.

A famous fictitious death occurred in the grounds of Exeter College: in Colin Dexter's *The Remorseful Day*, Inspector Morse collapses from a fatal heart attack in the front quadrangle to the accompaniment of Faure's *In Paradisium*.

Famous alumni and fellows: Writers J.R.R. Tolkien, Alan Bennett, Martin Amis, Will Self and Philip Pullman; former president Kufuor of Ghana; Nobel Laureate Sydney Brenner; proto-geologist Sir Charles Lyell; historian J.A. Froude; leading pre-Raphaelites William Morris and Edward Burne-Jones; film-maker Tariq Ali; athlete Roger Bannister; broadcasters Ned Sherrin and Russell Harty; actor Richard Burton.

Green Templeton College, Woodstock Road

Alternative names: Originally two separate foundations, Green College and Templeton College.

Founders (or, rather, chief benefactors): Dr Cecil and Ida Green (Green College, 1979), Sir John Templeton (Templeton College, renamed 1984, originally the non-collegiate Oxford Centre for Management Studies (OCMS), est. 1965). When it comes to naming official founders, these three are usually joined by Clifford Barclay, Sir Norman Chester, Professor Sir Richard Doll and Norman Leyland.

College secrets: Green College was based around the eighteenth-century buildings centred on the Radcliffe Observatory. Templeton, based at Egrove Park in Kennington, came into being after Sir John Templeton gave the Oxford Centre for Management Studies one of the largest cash-inputs ever made to a British educational establishment.

Green College, before the benefactions of Dr and Mrs Green, was going to be called Radcliffe College: the foundation was authorised under this name in 1977.

Templeton College found its benefactor in 1982 when Uwe Kitzinger, Director of OCMS, published a begging article in *The American Oxonian* entitled 'A college in search of a founder?' Fund manager and former Rhodes

Scholar John Templeton and his wallet stepped forward, one of his conditions for the $5 million input being that the institution should be renamed after his parents (not him, note!)

The college coat of arms features an image of the sun behind the astronomical symbol for Venus. This is a homage to the observation of the transit of Venus across the sun in 1761, a cosmological event that led to the building of the Radcliffe Observatory. There was nowhere in Britain to view the phenomenon properly, and Oxford astronomers were keen never to be caught out again.

Famous alumni and fellows: Kunal Basu, author; Dame Valerie Beral, epidemiologist; Sanjaya Lall, economist; Peter Friend, surgeon; Derrick Gosselin, engineer and economist; Stein Ringen, sociologist; Rosemary Stewart, business theorist; Sir Crispin Tickell, diplomat and environmentalist; Michael von Clemm, businessman, restaurateur, anthropologist.

Harris Manchester College, Mansfield Road

Alternative names: Manchester Academy and Harris College; Latin *Collegium de Harris et Manchester.*

Founder: Originally founded by Presbyterian committee in 1757. The modern version was founded in 1990 by committee, named after benefactor Major Charles Harris MC. It became a full collegiate member of the university in 1996.

College secrets: Originally founded as Warrington Academy, 1757, it was re-founded in Manchester as the Manchester Academy in 1786. In 1803 the college moved to York, and back to Manchester in 1840, before migrating to London in 1853 and becoming a Collegiate Society of the University of London. In 1889, when changes in the law meant that students were no longer required to be

Anglicans, it decided to join the University of Oxford, but had to wait 100 years to realise this ambition.

The college's first purpose-built buildings were designed by Thomas Worthington in 1893. It is the smallest of the Oxford colleges, and claims to be 'Oxford's friendliest college'.

Harris Manchester has always supported socially progressive causes, such as anti-slavery, emancipation and workers' rights. In the early twentieth century it ran courses for the Workers' Educational Association.

The college's Tate Library, sixth largest in the university, was built by Sir Henry Tate of London's Tate Gallery fame. The college chapel has stained-glass windows by Pre-Raphaelites Edward Burne-Jones and William Morris.

Famous alumni and fellows: John Dalton, eighteenth-century atomic theorist; High Court Judge Oliver Popplewell; sub-minute mile runner Roger Bannister (fellow); Lord Nicholas Charles Edward Jonathan Windsor, youngest son of the Duke and Duchess of Kent; MP Jocelyn Davies; Colombian MP and anti-corruption activist Ingrid Betancourt Pulecio; journalist Maurizio Molinari.

Hertford College, Catte Street

Alternative names: The Principal, Fellows, and Scholars of Hertford College in the University of Oxford; Latin *Collegium Hertfordiense.*

Founders: Elias de Hertford, 1280 (Hart Hall) and Dr Richard Newton, 1740 (the first Hertford College).

College secrets: The college motto, *Sicut cervus anhelat AD fontes aquarum,* translates as 'As the hart panteth after the water brooks'.

The institution was founded in 1282 as Hart Hall (or *Aula Cervina* in Latin), the original building being where Hertford's late sixteenth-century Old Hall is today.

The Secret History of Oxford

Leased to Exeter College, it was not allowed to blossom as an independent hall/college until much later.

Funds had dried up by 1810 and the college was dissolved. In 1822 its site and assets were annexed by Magdalen Hall, whose own site had suffered a disastrous fire the previous year. This hall was founded in 1448 by William of Waynflete, ten years before he founded Magdalen College. In 1874 Magdalen Hall was dissolved and the new Hertford College came into being via Act of Parliament.

Vice-Principal Hewitt was the last fellow of the original, doomed Hertford College. When his fellowship expired in 1818, he had been 'Fellow without a college' for thirteen years.

171 members of Hertford College died during the two world wars in the twentieth century, including Major Percy Nugent FitzPatrick, killed near Cambrai in 1917. It was his father, James Percy FitzPatrick, who first suggested that a two-minute silence should be kept each year at 11 a.m. on the 11th of the 11th – Armistice Day.

Hertford has a college cat, Simpkin, the ninth in a line of cats, all called Simpkin. He lives in the college lodge and is provided with a bursary by college alumni, which covers food and vet bills. It remains to be seen whether or not this ninth incarnation is using the last of Simpkin's nine lives.

Famous alumni and fellows: 'Metaphysical' poet John Donne; author Jonathan Swift; Henry Pelham, Prime Minister 1743–54; Whig bigwig Charles James Fox (all Hart Hall); philosopher Thomas Hobbes; Bible translator William Tyndale; politician Edward Hyde, Earl of Clarendon (all Magdalen Hall); philosopher Alain Locke; Prime Minister of Malta Dom Mintoff (1955–58, 1971–84); TV presenters Fiona Bruce, Krishnan Guru-Murthy and Natasha Kaplinsky; authors Gavin *Ring of Bright Water*

Maxwell and Evelyn Waugh. Charles Ryder, the hero in Waugh's novel *Brideshead Revisited* went to Hertford, like his creator.

Jesus College, Turl Street

Alternative names: Jesus College in the University of Oxford of Queen Elizabeth's Foundation.

Founders: Not Elizabeth (as that alternative name would seem to imply) but Hugh Aprice (or Price) in 1571. He was a Welsh clergyman educated at Oxford, the most prominent of the college's eight Welsh founding fathers – largely because he had the money to make the foundation financially sound. Elizabeth accepted the honorary title of founder from him, and the college owns three portraits of her.

College secrets: Jesus College replaced an earlier foundation on the same site, White Hall, which had existed since the thirteenth century.

Between 1571 and 1915 the college's succession of twenty-four Principals all came from Wales or were of Welsh descent, the one exception being Cornish (and therefore still Celtic) Francis Howell, 1657-1660.

You might think Welsh was the language of choice in such a self-consciously Welsh-oriented college. However, college statutes from 1622 show that 'public conversation' in class, hall or quadrangle, was forbidden in any language other than Latin, Greek or Hebrew. Modern St David's Day (1 March) celebrations at the college centre on Welsh sermons and speeches, however.

The St David's Day Dinner features a unique dish, Sir Watkin Williams-Wynn's Pudding. It is named after an eighteenth-century Jacobite (i.e. pro-Stuart monarchy during the Georgian era), Welsh politician and alumni of the college.

Williams-Wynn also donated a silver-gilt punch bowl to the college. Tradition maintains that the bowl can be claimed by anyone who can meet these two challenges: putting their arms around its widest point (1.57m) and then draining it of strong punch. Contenders occasionally succeed in the former challenge but the second is impossible, not to mention suicidal, as the bowl is capable of holding 80 pints (45 litres) when full.

The college's undergraduate 'newspaper' enjoys the title *The Sheepshagger.*

Famous alumni and fellows: Second Keeper of the Ashmolean Edward Lluyd; historians Sir Goronwy Edwards, J.R. Green and Lord (Robert) Skidelsky; T.E. Lawrence 'of Arabia'; founder and president of the African National Congress Pixley ka Isaka Seme; Chief Minister of Jamaica Norman Washington Manley; Prime Minister Harold Wilson; poets Henry Vaughan, Goronwy Owen, Gwyn Thomas and Dom Moraes; novelist William Boyd; Mastermind quiz-master Magnus Magnusson; and Ffion Jenkins, wife of MP William Hague.

Keble College, Parks Road

Alternative names: Latin *Collegium Keblense.*

Founder: Founded by committee in 1870, the most notable member being Edward Pusey, Professor at Christ Church College, and the leading thinker of the Anglo-Catholic Oxford Movement, aka the Tractarians, after their journal *Tract of the Times.* The college was named in memory of John Keble (1792–1866), founding member of the Tractarians.

College secrets: The college was funded by Tractarian sympathisers. These included William Gibbs, whose cash was derived from the guano (bird-droppings) industry in Peru. The guano was sold as a valuable fertiliser, and commanded a high price in those pre-chemical nitrates days.

Architect William Butterfield (1814-1900) stated he 'had a mission to give dignity to brick'. He was an exponent of the Gothic style, but his translation of those ideas into brick did not meet mass approval. Keble was nicknamed the Holy Zebra by fans and foes alike, on account of its brickwork 'stripes'. It is worth remembering that the anti-Tractarians would have criticised anything erected by their Anglo-Catholic enemies.

The founders had decreed 'poverty and obedience' as prerequisites for their students. Human nature thwarted this, and the college was chided for its unlicensed boxing matches, at which 'the liquid refreshment was not tea' as one nineteenth-century commentator delicately put it.

In 1871 Keble became the first college to issue stamps for delivering messages. Other Oxford colleges followed suit, until the service was undermined by the national efforts of the Post Office in 1886. Proof, once again, that philately will get you nowhere.

Famous alumni and fellows: Historians Geoffrey Hill and Dame Averil Cameron; writers Giles Coren, Angela Saini and Humphrey Carpenter; Judge James Hunt; politicians Ed Balls, Richard Harrington and Arthur Dyke Acland; cricketer Imran Khan; Newfoundland Premier Danny Williams; Samaritans founder Chad Varah.

Kellogg College, Banbury Road

Alternative name: Formerly Rewley House.

Founder: The Kellogg foundation, 1990 (when it was named Rewley House). It achieved full college status and the Kellogg tag in 1994.

College secrets: The Kellogg Foundation, upon whose money the college is founded, has a broad remit to support 'good causes'. It is separate from the famous cornflake manufacturer, but both were founded by Will Keith Kellogg, a cereal money-maker.

Kellogg is the most recent of all the Oxford colleges. All its students are graduates, and many study part-time while furthering their careers. This makes the college self-consciously 'worldly', serving the business community (it is home to the Oxford Centre for Mutual and Employee-Owned Business) and other professionals such as creative writers.

Rewley House was built in 1873 as a convent school, St Anne's Rewley, named after the thirteenth-century Rewley Abbey which once stood nearby. Kellogg College moved to a new site on Banbury Road in the late 1890s. The original building now houses the Oxford University Department for Continuing Education, one of the largest university departments.

Famous alumni and fellows: Computer scientist Sir Charles Antony Richard Hoare; businessman and pharmacologist Sir Ralph Kohn; writers P.D. James and Prajwal Parajuly; historian I. Joan Thirsk; human rights lawyers Juan E. Mendez and Geraldine Van Bueren; film producer David Puttnam; writer and philosopher Umberto Eco (honorary fellow).

Lady Margaret Hall, Norham Gardens

Alternative name: LMH.

Founder: Edward Talbot, Warden of Keble College, and his wife Lavinia, 1878.

College secrets: Founded as the first college for women in Oxford, with just nine students, in 1879. It was not incorporated into the university until 1913.

Named after Lady Margaret Beaufort (1443–1509), mother of King Henry VII (and therefore of the Tudor dynasty) and patron of education and scholarship.

The college coat of arms is a concise summary of its origins: a portcullis echoes the family arms of Lady Margaret Beaufort, three Talbot dogs (an extinct hunting breed, forerunner of the beagle and bloodhound) represent founder Edward Talbot, and the bell is a family symbol of the hall's first Principal, Elizabeth Wordsworth.

The hall's chapel was designed by Giles Gilbert Scott, who designed such English icons as Battersea Power Station, Liverpool Cathedral and the traditional red telephone box. He was the son of George Gilbert Scott, who designed the Martyr's Memorial on St Giles in Oxford.

The hall's latest library, dedicated to law, was built beneath the existing library. It was opened in 2006 by Cherie Booth, QC and wife of former PM Tony Blair.

Famous alumni and fellows: Formula One commentator James Allen; writers Gertrude Bell, Lindsey Davis, Antonia Fraser and Elizabeth Longford; playwright Caryl Churchill; folklorist and writer Katherine Briggs; assassinated Pakistan premier Benazir Bhutto; politicians Ann Widdecombe, Matthew Taylor and Michael Gove; photojournalist Tim Hetherington; founder of the BBC Sound Archive Marie Slocombe; Save the Children founder Eglantyne Jebb; celebrity chef Nigella Lawson; comedian Josie Long; athlete Ben Moreau; actors Diana Quick and Samuel West.

Linacre College, St Cross Road

Alternative name: Originally Linacre House, home of the Linacre Society, before becoming a university college in 1986.

Founder: Founded by committee, 1962, with Principal John Bamborough foremost in their ranks. Named after Renaissance scholar and All Souls alumni Thomas Linacre (*c.*1460–1524), humanist, medical scientist and founder of the Royal College of Physicians (Henry VIII being his most high-profile patient).

College secrets: The original Linacre House is now the Music Department of Oxford University on St Aldates.

The university's Linacre Chair of Zoology predates the college. The Professorship was founded in 1860, named after Thomas Linacre, with origins in the Linacre Lectureships at Merton College 300 years earlier.

The college consists of fellows and postgraduates – there are no undergraduates.

Linacre was the first Oxford college to achieve Fairtrade status, in March 2011.

Linacre's current site on Banbury Road is named Ursula Hicks House, after Lady Ursula Hicks, a founding fellow who bequeathed her home to the college. The home was sold, but her name lives on.

Famous alumni and fellows: Anthropologist and first Peruvian Minister of Culture Juan Ossio Acuña; astronomer and TV presenter Heather Couper; literary critic Terry Eagleton; journalist and South African politician Frene Ginwala; Olympic gold medallist rower Jake Wetzel; BBC presenter Yan Wong; Nobel Prize-winning biochemist and president of the Royal Society Sir Paul Nurse; Nobel Prize-winning economist Sir John Hicks; economist and founder of The Review of Economic Studies Lady Ursula Hicks.

Lincoln College, Turl Street

Alternative name: 'The College of the Blessed Mary and All Saints, Lincoln, in the University of Oxford, commonly called Lincoln College'.

Founder: Richard Fleming, Bishop of Lincoln, 1427.

College secrets: The college was poor for much of its early history, which has actually been good for posterity: with no money to knock things down and rebuild, the old college is beautifully preserved.

The founder planned to equip orthodox clergy with the religious and philosophical insights to crush the Lollard heresy. Lollardy was one of the early attempts to question the doctrine of the Catholic church. Lincoln College, Fleming declared, would be a 'little college of true students of theology who would defend the mysteries of Scripture against those ignorant laymen who profaned with swinish snouts its most holy pearls'.

Much of the famous *King James Bible* (1611) was translated into English at the college, a task spearheaded by Lincoln men Richard Kilby and Richard Brett.

Methodism founder John Wesley formulated much of his spiritual and practical thinking in the precincts of Lincoln. The college can rightly claim to have been the place from which the Methodist Church sprang.

The building containing Oxford's famous pub The Mitre belongs to the college. The former All Saints' Church, opposite The Mitre, has been the college library since 1971. The church was opened in 1708, following the collapse of the older version in 1699. The tower and spire are sometimes said to be the work of Christopher Wren, but this is not the case. The architect is unknown, although Nicholas Hawksmoor appears to have been involved.

Famous alumni and fellows: Lutenist and composer Francis Pilkington; playwright and Poet Laureate William Davenant; physician and Oxford icon John Radcliffe; revolutionary churchman John Wesley; developers of antibiotics Lord Howard Florey (Nobel Prize winner for his role in developing penicillin) and Sir Edward Abraham; children's writer Theodore Geisel, aka Dr Seuss; author David Cornwell, aka John le Carré; racing driver Will Bratt.

Magdalen College, High Street

Alternative name: The President and Fellows of the College of St Mary Magdalen in the University of Oxford; Latin *Collegium Beatae Mariae Magdalenae.*

Magdalen College.

Founder: William of Waynflete, Lord Chancellor and Bishop of Winchester, 1458.

College secrets: Although founded in 1458, building work did not start until 1467. This was due to the uncertainty brought about by the Wars of the Roses, namely the civil strife that resulted in the Tudors ascending the throne in 1485.

The iconic bell tower at the western end of the High Street took seventeen years to complete, between 1492 and 1509. On the morning of 1 May each year, choristers sing from the top of the tower. They have been doing this since 1509. The original concert was a memorial for Henry VII, who had died that year. Since the late eighteenth century, choristers have sung the *Te Deum patrem collimus*, the Magdalen College hymn. This tradition began one wet May Morning, when choristers were unable to read their soaked music. All they could muster between them from memory was the *Te Deum*.

In the civil wars of the seventeenth century, the bell tower was used as a lookout post by the Royalists, and as an elevated spot for catapulting stones at the enemy. In the war's aftermath, victorious Parliamentarians Cromwell and Fairfax dined here and received honorary degrees. They were supposed to sit and listen to learned debate, but opted instead for a game of bowls outside.

Christ Church Meadow with old city wall and Magdalen Bell Tower. (Photograph by Jan Sullivan)

Magdalen has won *University Challenge* (the TV quiz show, running since 1962) four times – more than any other institution.

Famous alumni and fellows: Cardinals Thomas Wolsey and Reginald Pole; historian and MP Edward Gibbon; former Prime Ministers Malcolm Fraser (Australia) and John Turner (Canada); film director Terrence Malick; zoologist and writer Desmond Morris; journalists and TV presenters John Sergeant and Louis Theroux; actors Dudley Moore and Robert Hardy; journalist and TV presenter Ian Hislop; poets John Betjemen and Seamus Heaney; writers Oscar Wilde, C.S. Lewis, Alan Hollingshurst and Julian Barnes; Kings Edward VIII (UK) and Jigme Wangchuck (Bhutan); politicians Lord Alfred Denning, William Hague and George Osborne.

Mansfield College, Mansfield Road

Alternative name: Originally Spring Hill College, Birmingham, founded 1838.

Founder: By committee, 1886, at the instigation of Prime Minister William Gladstone, and named after George and Elizabeth Mansfield, the foundation's principle donors.

College secrets: The college moved to Oxford from its previous base in Birmingham in 1886, shedding its original name in the process. It became a permanent private hall of the University of Oxford in 1955. In 1995 it received the Royal Charter that allowed it to make the final leap and become a fully paid-up member of the college system.

Its original purpose was to provide further education and theological training for nonconformist ministers, and to provide a focal point for dissenters previously excluded from the religious life of the university. Prior to 1871, people from Christian denominations other than the

Church of England were unable to take degrees. William Gladstone changed this law and advocated the establishment of a non-conformist college in Oxford.

Although no longer a religious institution (the last United Reformed Church-sponsored course ran in 2006), the college's principles are still informed by its grounding in freedom of conscience and wider educational access. Having said that, chapel services are still Nonconformist in structure, and the college chaplain is chosen from Nonconformist contenders.

Portraits in the college hall celebrate the original 1662 Dissenters and the leading names of the tradition, including Oliver Cromwell and John Hampden.

Former college porter Hugh Flint played drums on the first two John Mayall & the Bluesbreakers albums, and went on to form the band McGuinness Flint.

Famous alumni and fellows: Adam von Trott, member of the German resistance in the Second World War; philosopher Pamela Sue Anderson; MPs Chris Bryant and Charles Silvester Horne; pianist Paul Crossley; producer and writer Adam Curtis; prosecutor during the Hutton Inquiry James Dingemans QC; anarchist writer and activist Uri Gordon; journalists Stephen Pollard, Justin Rowlatt, Michael Pollan and Peter Hessler; poet and theologian Amos Wilder.

Merton College, Merton Street

Alternative name: The House or College of Scholars of Merton in the University of Oxford.

Founder: Walter de Merton, Chancellor of England under Henry III and Edward I, also Bishop of Rochester, 1264.

College secrets: The first University College – it housed scholars who worked to achieve academic ends, whereas the earlier halls had merely provided accommodation.

Merton College Chapel gargoyles. (Photograph by Jan Sullivan)

Merton has the oldest continuously functioning university library in the world, Mob Library. The original books were kept in locked chests, and the library still has medieval volumes chained to the shelves (a heavyweight theft-deterrent in an age when books were literally irreplaceable).

The Gatehouse was built in the early fifteenth century when King Henry V granted the college a 'license to crenellate', which meant they could construct battlements. This was only granted to a trusted few, as crenellations implied defence, which meant potential to provide a stronghold for rebel barons in times of insurrection.

The college chapel is a treasure house. Featuring architectural work by Christopher Wren, Edward Blore, William Butterfield and Sir Gilbert Scott, it also contains thirteenth-century windows and a lectern from 1504, reckoned one of the best pre-Reformation survivals in the country.

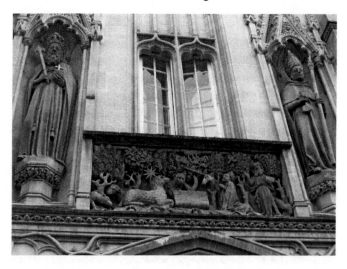

Merton College fresco. (Photograph by Jan Sullivan)

Staunchly Catholic under Queen Mary I in the sixteenth century, Merton and its chapel withstood a siege against the officers of Queen Elizabeth's Church police for three weeks, refusing to forsake its Catholic paraphernalia.

In 1717 the back door to Merton Gardens was permanently closed, as it was being used as a rendezvous by students and 'young ladies'.

Merton's newest addition is the organ, installed in 2013 to replace the 1960s model. It was built by Dobson Pipe Organ Builders of Lake City, Iowa.

Japanese Crown Prince Naruhito carried out postgraduate research on the history of Thames transportation in 1983–84. This unlikely marriage is the theme of his book *The Thames and I: A Memoir of Two Years at Oxford.*

Famous alumni and fellows: Bodleian founder Sir Thomas Bodley (the new library at Merton was his inspiration); seventeenth-century physician William Harvey; Winston's father Lord Randolph Churchill; J.R.R.

Tolkien, Merton Professor of English Language and Literature 1945–59; Nobel Prize-winning poet T.S. Eliot; RAF pilot and philanthropist Leonard Cheshire; engineer and mountaineer Andrew 'Sandy' Irvine, who joined George Mallory's doomed Mount Everest expedition in 1924 and whose body has never been found; Nobel Prize-winning physicist Sir Anthony Leggett; Nobel Prize-winning behavioural zoologist Nikolaas Tinbergen; Nobel Prize-winning chemist Frederick Soddy; mathematician Sir Andrew Wiles who, in 1994, proved Fermat's Last Theorem, which had been causing headaches for 350 years; Director-General of the BBC Mark Thompson.

New College, Holywell Street

Alternative name: 'The Warden and Scholars of St Mary's College of Winchester in Oxford, commonly called New College in Oxford'. It was known as New College from the earliest days, to distinguish it from Oxford's other college named after Mary, Oriel.

Founder: William of Wykeham, bishop of Winchester, 1379.

College secrets: The college was built on cut-price land formerly occupied by the city dunghill, notorious as a prostitutes' rendezvous.

The enclosed Front Quad, dating from 1386, set the trend: all other colleges, at Oxford and elsewhere, followed the quadrangle pattern afterwards. The Front Quad's third storey was added in the 1670s: you can see the join.

The college was founded at the same time as Winchester College, with the express function of providing trained and educated clergy to fill a church landscape emptied by the Black Death.

Amongst the 'hidden' treasures of the college are the sixty-two fourteenth-century misericords – carvings on the underside of seats – in the chapel choir stalls.

New College Gateway.

The college grounds include a perfectly preserved section of the medieval town walls. Founder William of Wykeham had agreed to look after the wall as a condition of using the land. Every three years Oxford's Lord Mayor and Corporation have to walk along the wall to check that Wykeham's heirs are fulfilling the obligation.

Famous alumni and fellows: Politicians Tony Benn, Harold Wilson, Gyles Brandreth, Hugh Gaitskell; father of spoonerisms William Spooner (fellow); biologists W.D. Hamilton, Richard Dawkins (fellows); philosopher Isaiah Berlin (fellow); actors Kate Beckinsale, Hugh Grant; TV personalities Angus Deayton, Nigel Rees; authors John Fowles, Patrick Gale, Naomi Wolfe, Kate Mosse, Sophie Kinsella; publisher Victor Gollancz; BBC Director General Alistair Milne; film directors Christopher James Hampton, Mel Smith, Florian Maria Georg Christian, Graf Henckel von Donnersmarck; cricketers Brian Johnson, Douglas Jardine; dramatist Dennis Potter; journalists Rageh Omar, Tim Sebastian.

Nuffield College, New Road

Founder: William Morris (Lord Nuffield), 1937.

College secrets: Nuffield scored many firsts: the first college to have subject specialisation (social sciences in this case), the first to admit male and female students and academics, and the first graduate-only college in the university.

The college buildings were designed by Austen Harrison. His original plans, inspired by Mediterranean models, were rejected by the founder, who wanted something more in keeping with the very English surroundings.

The site was a disused Oxford canal basin with coal wharfs. The original plans had to be scaled down due to problems with budget and lack of materials in post-war Britain. The 'temporary' car park over the road from the college is a lingering result of this shortfall – it only exists because the college was unable to extend its sprawl westwards over Worcester Street.

Morris's plans were approved in 1940. Though work finally began in 1949 the college was not completed until 1960. Originally funded solely by Morris, in the late 1950s the Nuffield Foundation charity was set up to provide more funding.

The college is pre-eminent in economics and politics, notably psephology, the scientific analysis of elections. Morris himself was not entirely happy with the shape the college's academic character had taken, describing it famously as 'that bloody Kremlin... where left-wingers study at my expense.'

The no-nonsense green spire of Nuffield is actually a masonry-clad steel-framed library, containing the college's main book-stack.

Famous alumni and fellows: Manmohan Singh, Indian Prime Minister; Mark Carney, Governor of the Bank of Canada and Governor-designate of the Bank of England; Nicholas Stern, Senior Vice-President of the World Bank; Sir Gus O'Donnell, British senior civil servant; Kofi Abrefa Busia, Prime Minister of Ghana; MPs Richard Bruton, Donald Chapman (Baron Northfield), Patricia Hewitt; Geoffrey Gallop, former Premier of Western Australia; John Kay, economist and columnist; Martin Wolf, chief economics correspondent of the *Financial Times.*

Oriel College, Oriel Square

Alternative name: 'The Provost and Scholars of the House of the Blessed Mary the Virgin in Oxford, commonly called Oriel College, of the Foundation of Edward the Second of famous memory, sometime King of England.'

Founder: Adam de Brome, under the patronage of Edward II, 1324. Brome was rector of the university church, and the king's almoner (someone who distributed alms to the poor).

College secrets: The college swallowed up earlier medieval halls, including Perilous Hall, Bedel Hall,

St Mary Hall, St Martin Hall and Tackley's Inn. The latter, fronting the High Street, is the oldest surviving medieval hall in Oxford.

The college also purchased La Oriole, a crown property. The name of that older building somehow stuck to the college – very early on, too; it seems to have been known by this name in 1349. 'Oriel' or 'oriole' refers to the oratoriolum or oriel window which was, clearly, a major feature of this building. An oriel is a bay window which projects from a building without touching the ground.

Bartlemas is an area of the college incorporating parts of a leper hospital founded by Henry I (*d.* 1135).

In the centre of the O'Brien Quad is a 'real tennis' court, a sixteenth-century version of the game featuring a walled court, with a sloping roof on three of the walls. Both Charles I and Edward VII played tennis here (not at the same time).

Oriel's Rhodes Building was constructed in 1911 with money given by former student Cecil Rhodes (see p.166). The High Street frontage has statues of Rhodes, Edward VII and George V. Rhodes can also be seen in a metal plaque on the wall of No.6 King Edward Street. This thoroughfare was created by Oriel in 1873 following the demolition of two large buildings on the High Street.

Famous alumni and fellows: Thomas Arundel, who crowned Henry IV in 1367; historians Eric Foner, Christopher Hibbert, A.J.P. Taylor, Michael Wood; poets Mathew Arnold, Norman Cameron, David Wright; mathematician John Nunn; naturalist Gilbert White; writers Michael Innes, Richard Hughes, Herman Merivale, Eric Schlosser; dramatist Peter Harness; business guru Phillip Oppenheim; 'Oxford Movement' main men John Henry Newman, John Keble and Edward Bouverie Pusey.

Pembroke College, St Aldates

Alternative name: The Master, Fellows, and Scholars of Pembroke College, Latin *Collegium Pembrochianum.* Originally Broadgates Hall, a hostel for law students.

Founders: Abingdon burgesses Thomas Tesdale, merchant, and Richard Wightwick, clergyman, 1624. The college was named after William Herbert, 3rd Earl of Pembroke and Chancellor of the university. His heraldic arms, three lions, appear on the college's badge.

College secrets: The college was originally founded to provide places at Oxford for boys from Abingdon School.

Pembroke Master Bartholomew Price, fellow of the Royal Society, listed his recreations in *Who's Who* as 'none in particular'. He is remembered, bizarrely, more for his nickname 'the Bat', which was the basis of Lewis Carroll's 'Twinkle Twinkle little bat, how I wonder what you're at' in *Alice in Wonderland.*

Sir Roger Bannister, Master of the College in 1985, is known for being the first man to run 1 mile in under one minute, at Iffley Road track on 6 May 1954. But he was, first and foremost, a noted neurologist, and oversaw the completion of the Sir Geoffrey Arthur Building.

Samuel Johnson's former rooms at the college are pointed out on tours (on the second storey above the college main entrance). He entered Pembroke College in 1728 in great poverty and left just over a year later when the condition failed to correct itself. Johnson never finished his degree, but Oxford University awarded him with an honorary one in 1775.

Famous alumni and fellows: historian and writer William Camden; writers Samuel Johnson and William Shenstone; lawyer Sir William Blackstone; founder of the Smithsonian Institution James Smithson (illegitimate son of the first Duke of Northumberland); co-founder, with the Wesleys, of

Methodism, George Whitefield; Rawlinson and Bosworth Professor in Anglo-Saxon at Pembroke 1926–45, J.R.R. Tolkien; philosopher Robin George Collingwood; MP Michael Heseltine; King Abdullah II of Jordan; foreign minister of Poland Radek Sikorski; Prime Minister of Hungary Viktor Orbán; TV wine man Oz Clarke.

The Queen's College, High Street

Alternative name: Hall of the Queen's Scholars at Oxford;. or The Provost and Scholars of The Queen's College in the University of Oxford; Latin *Collegium Reginae*. It was Queen's Hall or Queenhall before it became The Queen's College. It is usually shorted to Queen's.

Founder: Robert de Eglesfield, 1341.

College secrets: Named after Philippa of Hainault, Edward III's Queen. The founder was her chaplain.

Robert de Eglesfield's memory is kept alive in a surviving Queen's feast, the Needle and Thread Gaudy. College members new to the fold are given a needle and thread (*auguille* and *fil* in French, sounding a bit like 'eagle' and 'field', as in 'Egles'-field). The token item is supposed to help mend one's college garments, and is handed over with the injunction to be thrifty. The punning eagles are present on the college coat of arms, and can be spied by the eagle-eyed in some of the college carvings too.

The Baroque character of Queen's was largely the work of Nicholas Hawksmoor in the eighteenth century, when the decision was taken to give the medieval college a drastic facelift.

For many centuries the college consisted largely of scholars from Cumberland, Westmorland and Yorkshire. The lavish Boar's Head Feast (see p.210) originated as a banquet for students who could not get home over the Christmas period, it being such a long way to travel.

Famous alumni and fellows: King Henry V; fourteenth-century church revolutionary John Wycliffe; Jacobean playwright Thomas Middleton; philosopher Jeremy Bentham; actor Rowan Atkinson; MP Ruth Kelly; psychoanalyst Wilfred Bion; astronomers Edward 'Comet' Halley and Edwin Powell 'Telescope' Hubble; Thai Prime Minister Mom Rajawongse Kukrit Pramoj; neurologist and writer Oliver Sacks; World Wide Web inventor Tim Berners-Lee.

Regent's Park College, Pusey Street

Alternative name: Regent's; Latin *Collegium de Principis Cum Regentis Paradiso.* Previously Stepney Academy.

Founder: Founded by committee. The man who arranged Regent's transition to Oxford was H. Wheeler Robinson, Principal of the college while it was still in London.

College secrets: It was a Baptist church foundation originally, and retains an informality that stems from these roots. Unlike most colleges, there are no separate dining facilities for academic and support staff; everyone eats together in the main dining hall. Sounds normal, but in the collegiate system it is anything but.

The college's first incarnation was as the London Baptist Education Society, 1752. It moved to Stepney in 1810 and Regent's Park in 1855, at which point it was part of the University of London. It became part of Oxford University in 1957.

Regent's has two unique special collections: the 'Angus Library and the Archive of the life and history of Baptists and nonconformists from the late fifteenth century to the present day' and the 'David Nicholls Memorial Collection', concerning the politics and history of Haiti.

Famous alumni and fellows: Judge Malcolm Bishop; author the Revd Simon Bailey; religious broadcaster the Revd Wayne Clarke; comedian Steve Hall; poets Tamsin Kendrick and Michael Symmons Roberts; Alexandra Knatchbull, descendant of Queen Victoria and god-daughter of Diana, Princess of Wales; novelists Gregory Norminton and T. Davis Bunn; Dhirendra Sahu, Lord Bishop of Eastern Himalaya; child actor and writer James Gandhi.

St Anne's College, Woodstock Road

Alternative names: Latin *Collegium Santae Annae,* formerly the Society of Home-Students, and the St Anne's Society.

Founder: As it says on the college's website, 'St Anne's, in 1879, was not so much founded as invented... a manifesto rather than a location.' In 1942, the Society of Home-Students became the St Anne's Society, and a fully-fledged college in 1952.

College secrets: The site of the new college was formerly an ancient meadow, St Giles Fields, belonging to St John's College.

The first space occupied by the Society of Home Students was a common room on Ship Street. The college's alumni magazine is still called *The Ship.*

The concept that eventually became the college was founded by a radical-minded group who believed that women should be given the opportunity to study in Oxford without having to belong to one of the old patriarchal colleges. This concept allowed women to lodge in the city and take courses by attending university lectures and tutorials, which would make studying relatively affordable.

The first St Anne's degrees were not handed out until 1920.

Grace Hadow, College Principal 1929–1940, was ambivalent about her new library (1938) and its dedicated students: 'I am really rather horrified to find that the new library is attracting people so much that even on fine sunny afternoons it is full of young women industriously reading.' In the Second World War the library's Fulford Room became a highly productive munitions factory.

When wolves escaped from the former Oxford Zoo, women from St Anne's were advised to carry umbrellas if they were venturing onto the streets, to general hilarity.

Famous alumni and fellows: Actress Maria Aitken; authors Zoë Heller, Karen Armstrong, Penelope Lively, Jill Paton Walsh, Diana Wynne Jones, Helen Fielding; journalists Melanie Phillips, Tina Brown and Gillian Reynolds; MPs Edwina Currie and Danny Alexander; anthropologist Mary Douglas; poet U.A. Fanthorpe; radio journalists Libby Purves and Martha Kearney; conductors Simon Rattle and Julian Gallant.

St Antony's College, Woodstock Road

Founder: Antonin Besse, French businessman, 1950. It became a member of the collegiate system in 1963.

College secrets: Although a recent foundation, the site of St Antony's is one of Oxford's most ancient areas of settlement. There is archaeological evidence here of Romano-British buildings, and traces of earlier Iron Age activity.

The oldest buildings at St Antony's used to operate as Holy Trinity Convent, a quirk of history thrown up by the High Church 'Oxford Movement'. Erected by the Society of the Holy and Undivided Trinity 1866–68, its founder Marian Rebecca Hughes (1817–1912) had, in 1841, been the first woman since the 1530s Reformation to take nuns' vows within the mainstream church in England. The convent moved out after the Second World War, during which the grounds had been commandeered by the navy (about as far from the sea as they could possibly get).

The first of the college's new buildings was completed in 1970 and named the Besse building, after the founder and his wife (who continued to support the foundation after her husband's death).

Work on a new Middle Eastern Studies building, The Middle East Centre or Softbridge Building, began in January 2013. The building was designed by Iraqi-British architect Zaha Hadid.

Reflecting the college's role as an international centre, it currently has 400 students from over sixty-seven countries.

Famous alumni and fellows: writer Anne Applebaum; politician and historian Shlomo Ben-Ami; BBC journalist Owen Bennett-Jones; playwright and novelist John Griffith Bowen; historians Sir Richard John Evans, Wolfgang Leonhard and Robert Gildea; American journalist and columnist Thomas Lauren Friedman; playwright and screenwriter Julian Mitchell; MP John Redwood; Colombian politician and former president Álvaro Uribe Vélez; editor, feminist and socialist Hilary Wainwright.

St Benet's Hall, St Giles

Alternative name: Latin *Aula Privata Sancti Benedicti.* Known as Benet's (short form of 'Benedict'). Prior to 1918 it was known successively as Hunter-Blair's Hall and Parker's Hall.

Founder: The Benedictine Order of monks, 1897. It became a permanent private hall in 1918.

The hall used to occupy No. 103 Woodstock Road, in a building that is now a guest-house. In 1904 it moved to Grindle's Hall in Beaumont Street, and then, in 1922 to its present site at Nos. 38 and 39 St Giles. Grindle's Hall was demolished in 1938 when the Oxford Playhouse theatre was built.

College secrets: One of Oxford University's six permanent private halls. These are governed by Christian church institutions rather than fellows (as is the case with the colleges). It is not part of the Collegiate system, along with fellow permanent private halls Regent's Park College, Wycliffe Hall, Campion Hall, Blackfriars and St Stephen's House.

The original students at St Benet's were Benedictine monks from Ampleforth Abbey in North Yorkshire.

Students do not have to be Catholic, but must be supportive of the monks' way of living.

St Benet's is the only constituent body of the university that still only admits men.

Notable Masters and fellows: Father James Forbes (Master 1964–1979) pottery expert and Knight of Malta; Father Henry Wansbrough (Master 1990–2004), editor of the New Jerusalem Bible; Werner Günter Adolf Jeanrond (Master 2012–present), theologian and writer; Brian Klug (fellow), editor and human rights activist; Harry Sidebottom (fellow) and Henry Mayr-Harting (Honorary fellow), authors and historians.

St Catherine's College, Manor Road

Alternative names: St Catz, or plain Catz.

Founder: Alan Louis Charles Bullock, Baron Bullock, 1962, a historian renowned for his biography *Adolf Hitler: A Study in Tyranny.*

College secrets: Originally a 'Delegacy', or non-collegiate organisation, run by the university. This pre-college incarnation was founded in 1868 to give poorer sections of society access to an Oxford education.

Originally based in a single room at the top of the Clarendon Building, Broad Street, it then moved to the Examination Schools (two rooms!), followed by another property (No. 74) on the High Street. In 1936 it moved to a new building (currently the university Music Faculty) in St Aldate's, on land sold by Christ Church. St Catherine's purchased its current site, part of Holywell Great Meadow, from Merton College in 1960.

The Delegacy became known as St Catharine's Club, named after St Catherine's Hall on Broad Street (now part of Hertford College). The Club was officially recognised by the university as St Catherine's Society in 1931. The original spelling 'Catharine' was the subject of hot debate, and was eventually changed to the more conventional 'Catherine'.

In 1875 Prime Minister William Gladstone donated 180 books as the foundation of the institution's first library.

Famous alumni and fellows: Writer and critic Michael Billington; former Pakistan president Farooq Leghari; Pakistan Prime Minister H.S. Suhrawardy; BBC Director-General John Birt; poets Euros Bowen, Adam Foulds; authors P.C. Wren, Joseph Heller, Simon Winchester, Jeanette Winterson, Jeremy Duns, Sam Llewellyn; actors Alice Eve, Emily Woof; mogul and philanthropist J. Paul Getty; Olympian athletes David Hemery, Matthew Pinsent; comedian and writer Richard Herring; politician Peter Mandelson; playwright David Rudkin; chemistry Nobel Laureate John E. Walker.

St Cross College, St Giles

Alternative names: Stx (written only). Latin *Collegium Sanctae Crucis.*

Founder: By Committee, 1965, with William van Heyningen as prime instigator and first Master.

College secrets: Named after St Cross Road, the site of the Old School House and single-storey hut that was the college's original base.

The college grew from the need to provide a base for university academics without college membership (506 of them in 1961). Only by belonging to a college can staff become fellows. Without that distinction, academics had no clout in the university's administration. Even more vitally, it also meant they lacked free dining rights at the university.

St Cross only admits graduates. Its first intake, in 1965, numbered five.

The lease on the college's buildings at St Giles runs out in 2980. The site is owned by Pusey House, an Oxford religious institution linked to Edward Bouverie Pusey and the Oxford Movement (see p.206)

A second quadrangle is due to be finished in 2015, in time for the college's semi-centennial celebrations.

Famous alumni and fellows: Olympic rower Tim Foster; mathematician John Kingman; Israeli novelist Aharon Appelfeld; Ashmolean Museum curator Ruth Barnes; anthropologist, author, and TV presenter Richard Rudgley; former Romanian Prime Minister Mihai Răzvan Ungureanu; Sultan of the Malaysian state of Kelantan Muhammad V of Kelantan; geneticist John Burn; children's author M.G. Harris; musicians Graham Wiggins and Pete Mathias; author and historian Diarmaid MacCulloch.

St Edmund Hall, Queen's Lane

Alternative names: The Principal, Fellows and Scholars of St Edmund Hall in the University of Oxford. Colloquially 'Teddy Hall'.

Founder: Original foundation unknown, with a date estimated at around 1236. It is named after St Edmund of Abingdon, Archbishop of Canterbury, who taught in a house on this site in the 1190s. It was run by Queen's College in the sixteenth century. The modern college's foundation was 1957.

College secrets: This is the sole survivor of the pre-college medieval halls which implies that it is the oldest institution catering for *in situ* undergraduates in any university. Although the earliest written record of the hall dates from 1317, it is likely that the institution is considerably older than this. As the last of the Aula

(Latin for halls), St Edmund Hall members are known as 'Aularians'.

Religious controversy: Hall Principal William Taylor was a champion of the Lollards (followers of proto-Protestant dissident and Oxford scholar John Wycliffe), and was burnt at the stake for heresy in 1423. Principal Peter Payne was also a follower of Wycliffe, but escaped the fate of Taylor by fleeing to Prague in 1413 and becoming a leading figure of the Protestant Hussite church.

Ironically, this controversy became pro-Catholic when the hall maintained allegiance to the Stuarts after the 'Glorious Revolution' and the forced abdication of James II in 1688. It refused to swear allegiance to the Hanoverian kings in the following century.

The hall's Old Library was built at the end of the seventeenth century. It was the first in Oxford to be designed with shelves along the walls, and the last to have chains as part of its fittings (to fasten precious books to the shelf).

The east window of the chapel, reconstructed in 1865, has stained glass by Edward Burne-Jones and William Morris.

Famous alumni and fellows: Eighteenth-century antiquarian and writer Thomas Hearne; comic book writer Dan Abnett; journalist and *Financial Times* editor Lionel Barber; rugby players Stuart Barnes, Hugo MacNeill; newsreader Anna Botting; author and biographer Douglas Botting; broadcasters Robin Day, Peter Day, Samira Ahmed, Jeremy Paxman (fellow); writer Amitav Ghosh; writer and Python Terry Jones; comedians John Wells, John Waldron, Al Murray.

St Hilda's College, Cowley Place

Alternative names: Originally St Hilda's Hall.

Founder: Dorothea Beale, Principal of the Cheltenham Ladies' College, 1893. Gained full college status in 1961.

College secrets: The college could not afford a coat of arms in 1926, and had to make do with a makeshift ammonite design by Edmund New. It bore the rather depressing legend *non frustra vixi,* 'I lived not in vain' which was never a popular motto. This was the emblem of the college until 1960 when a full coat of arms was granted. The motto was not included in the coat of arms, although it is still used occasionally.

The ammonite is associated with the college's namesake, seventh-century holy woman St Hilda, who is said to have turned Yorkshire serpents into stone. The coiled shells of the extinct fossil ammonite were, for many years, thought to be stone snakes. This explains the coiled snake on the coat of arms.

In 1910 the existence of female students was formally acknowledged at the university by the formation of the Delegacy for Women Students, and St Hilda's became a recognised society for female scholars. Not until 1920 were they finally permitted to become proper members of the university. St Hilda's became an Oxford University College in 1961.

The college was very vocal in women's suffrage from the movement's inception until full suffrage (the right to vote in elections) for women in 1928. The college's debating society was affiliated with the National Union of Women's Suffrage Societies, and all the prominent campaigners spoke at St Hilda's.

St Hilda's admitted its first men in 2008.

Famous alumni and fellows: TV journalist Zeinab Badawi; Princess Haya Bint Al Hussein; poets Wendy Cope, Jenny Joseph; writers Susanna Clarke, Catherine Heath, Val McDermid, Rosalind Miles, Barbara Pym; TV historian Bettany Hughes; biographer Hermione Lee; politician Gillian Shephard, Baroness Shephard of Northwold; musician Jacqueline Du Pré (honorary fellow).

St Hugh's College, St Margaret's Road

Alternative names: Latin *Collegium Sancti Hugonis.*

Founder: Elizabeth Wordsworth (great-niece of the famous poet William Wordsworth and daughter of the Bishop of Lincoln), 1886.

College secrets: Named after one of the founder's father's thirteenth-century predecessors, St Hugh of Lincoln (aka Hugh of Avalon). Oxford was, for many centuries, part of the Lincoln diocese.

The founder's aim was to help women 'who find the charges of the present halls at Oxford and Cambridge (even the most moderate) beyond their means.'

The college has ten and a half acres of gardens attached, which are reckoned by many to be the finest in all the colleges.

St Hugh's was requisitioned by the military in the Second World War and used as the Hospital for Head Injuries. Makeshift brick huts (demolished in 1952) acted as wards, with space for 300 beds. Between 1940 and 1945, over 13,000 servicemen and women were treated here. During this time the medical staff installed at St Hilda's made huge advances in medical interventions for head trauma. The mortality rate for such injuries fell from 90 per cent to 9 per cent.

Famous alumni and fellows: Writer, politician, economist Aung San Suu Kyi; politicians Barbara Castle, Caroline Jackson, Fiona Hall, Gregg McClymont; writer, philosopher G.E.M. Anscombe; Judge Heather Hallett; writers Joanna Trollope, Mary Renault, Patricia Duncker; singer June Tabor; art critic and librettist Myfanwy Piper; journalist Rowan Pelling.

St John's College, St Giles

Alternative names: Saint John Baptist College, Latin *Collegium Divi Joannis Baptistae.*

Founder: Sir Thomas White, rich London merchant and Lord Mayor of London, 1555.

College secrets: The founder was a Roman Catholic, and the college was originally established as a place to educate Catholics during the short-lived Counter-Reformation of Queen Mary I. The buildings on St Giles had belonged to the College of St Bernard, a Cistercian monastic foundation and place of study closed down during the Dissolution of the Monasteries. These original buildings surround the Front Quadrangle.

The college became rich as Oxford spread outwards in the nineteenth century: much of the land over which the growing suburbs sprawled belonged to the college. It owns most of St Giles, including the Eagle and Child and the Lamb and Flag pubs. The latter is actually run by the college. With endowments in excess of £313 million St John's is the wealthiest of the Oxford colleges.

The Dolphin Quadrangle was built in the early twentieth century on the site of the old Dolphin Inn.

The late twentieth-century Tommy White Quad was designed by Ove Arup and won the 1976 Concrete Society Award. As the name of the award might suggest, not everyone is enamoured of this particular Quad. It isn't even quadrangular, but an L-shaped building with a garden.

The most recent feature of St John's is Kendrew Quadrangle, opened in 2010. It is named after former college president Sir John Kendrew, Nobel Laureate and the college's chief benefactor in the twentieth century. The Quad reflects the times by taking energy from sustainable sources: the building is largely heated via solar panels, geothermal pipes and boilers fuelled with wood-chips from the college's private woodlands.

Famous alumni and fellows: Sixteenth-century priest and martyr Edmund Campion; seventeenth-century university Chancellor and Archbishop of Canterbury

William Laud; eighteenth-century agricultural pioneer Jethro Tull; writers A.E. Housman, Kingsley Amis, John Wain, Timothy Mo; poets A.E. Houseman, Robert Graves, Philip Larkin; former Prime Minister Tony Blair; writer, TV presenter Victoria Cohen; MPs David Heath, Rhodri Morgan; DJ David Simmons.

St Peter's College, New Inn Hall Street

Alternative names: The Master, Fellows and Scholars of the College of St Peter-le-Bailey.

Founder: Francis James Chavasse (1846–1928) and his son Christopher Maude Chavasse (1884–1962) later Bishop of Rochester, 1928. It became a permanent private hall of the university the following year, and gained full college status in 1961.

College secrets: The college was founded as a hostel to provide low-cost Oxford education/accommodation for students of limited means.

New Inn Hall, which once occupied the St Peter's site, housed the Oxford mint briefly – it was the place to which Charles II took all the university's silver during the Civil War, to be turned into Royalist coinage.

Following financial crisis in the 1930s the college was on the verge of closure. It was rescued by a large financial helping hand offered by dour philanthropist William Morris, who later founded Nuffield College.

During the Second World War, students from Westfield College in London were evacuated to St Peter's. This left no room for the residents of the college, who were doled out to other Oxford institutions.

The former church of St Peter-le-Bailey on New Inn Hall Street is the college chapel. Built in 1874, this is the third incarnation of St Peter's. It used to occupy ground which is now Bonn Square (its former cemetery – its Bone

Square, you could say). The 'le Bailey' tag refers to the nearby Norman castle (as in motte-and-bailey).

Famous alumni and fellows: Screenwriter Simon Beaufoy; cricketer Jamie Dalrymple; president of Ghana Edward Akufo-Addo; writer the Revd Wilbert Vere *Thomas the Tank Engine* Awdry; poet Peter Dale; River Cottage chef Hugh Fearnley-Whittingstall; BBC journalist Matt Frei; painter Kurt Jackson; film director Ken Loach; Bhutan heir-apparent Jigyel Ugyen Wangchuck; authors Mike Carey, Gareth Russell; actor Hugh Dancy; Canadian writer and evolutionary biologist Graham Bell.

St Stephen's House, Marston Street

Alternative names: Staggers.

Founder: Leaders of the Tractarian movement in Oxford, primarily Edward King, Regius Professor of Pastoral Theology in the University of Oxford and later Bishop of Lincoln, 1876.

College secrets: Originally occupied the site taken over by The New Bodleian (The Weston Library, as it will become in 2015). In 1919 it moved to Norham Gardens near the University Parks and in 1980 to its current building on Marston Street, which previously belonged to the Society of St John the Evangelist (aka the Cowley Fathers), founded by Richard Meux Benson. Became a permanent private hall of the university in 2003.

The foundation was named after St Stephen, obviously, but also in memory of a Tractarian priest called Stephen, cut down before his prime.

With old-fashioned monastic-type rules, (there is still a daily Mass and morning and evening prayer) the foundation was nevertheless an Anglican (albeit very 'High' church) institution prior to 2003. It now trains and teaches Christians from across the denominational spectrum.

Famous alumni and Principals: James Leo Schuster, Bishop of St John's in South Africa; David Hope, Bishop of Wakefield, Bishop of London and Archbishop of York; David Thomas, Provincial Assistant Bishop to the Church in Wales; Edwin Barnes, Bishop of Richborough; Andrew Burnham, Bishop of Ebbsfleet; composer Anthony Caesar; journalist A.N. Wilson.

Somerville College, Woodstock Road

Alternative names: Somerville Hall, prior to 1894.

Founders: Committee of liberal-minded reformists in 1879.

College secrets: Named in honour of self-taught Scottish mathematician and scientist Mary Somerville (1780–1872), as a place to champion, by example, first class higher education for women.

It sprang from the Association for the Higher Education of Women, which formed in 1878. The original group split due to religious differences, one half forming St Margaret Hall, the other bringing a liberal approach to Somerville, stating in pre-foundation discussions that 'no distinction will be made between students on the ground of their belonging to different religious denominations.' This was a big deal in those days.

The Somerville family arms and motto were adopted by the college, including what their website calls 'the notoriously untranslatable' motto *Donec rursus impleat orbem.*

The college's first Principal, Madeleine Shaw-Lefevre, noted in her diary, 'for the first few years two cows and a pig formed part of the establishment, but these were later replaced by a pony and a donkey which might be seen disporting themselves in the field, adding to the picturesque and homely character of the place.'

Famous alumni and fellows: Writers Vera Brittain, Margaret Forster, Iris Murdoch, Dorothy L. Sayers, Dame

Antonia Susan Duffy (A.S. Byatt), Michèle Roberts, Maggie Gee, Winifred Holtby, Rose Macaulay; geneticist Dame Kay Davies; linguist and TV presenter Susie Dent; philosopher Philippa Foot; Prime Ministers Indira Gandhi, Margaret Thatcher; politicians Helen Goodman, Margaret Jay, Baroness Jay of Paddington, Shirley Williams (Baroness Williams of Crosby); Nobel Prize-winning scientist Dorothy Hodgkin; singer Emma Kirkby; campaigner and TV presenter Esther Rantzen.

Trinity College, Broad Street

Alternative names: The College of the Holy and Undivided Trinity in the University of Oxford, of the Foundation of Sir Thomas Pope (Knight).

Founder: Sir Thomas Pope, 1555.

College secrets: The thirteenth-century monastic foundation Durham College was the basis of Trinity. It had provided a place of study for monks from the Benedictine Cathedral Church in Durham. It was so fit for purpose that the founding of Trinity entailed no new building work. The Old Library is, today, the sole surviving part of Durham College.

The name comes from the original dedication of Durham College, which was to the Trinity, the Virgin and St Cuthbert.

Founder Pope was Henry VIII's Treasurer of the Court of Augmentations, and handled the lands robbed from religious institutions after the Dissolution of the Monasteries. He became – surprise surprise – very rich in the process. It was under Catholic Mary I's patronage that he founded Trinity.

Pope's reasons for founding the college were not so much public spirited and academically inspired as personal and panicky. He had no children, and wished to be prayed for. As part of the foundation deal, members of the college offered prayers to ease his tribulations in the afterlife.

In 1618 college president Ralph Kettell built a cellar beneath the Durham College-era refectory, without bothering to consult a structural engineer. The Refectory collapsed, and the present hall had to be constructed.

Famous alumni and fellows: Art historian Kenneth Clark; explorer, spy and poet Sir Richard Burton; publisher and inventor of the Norrington Table of College Rankings Sir Arthur Norrington; writer and literary critic Sir Arthur Quiller-Couch; writer Simon Tolkien; eighteenth-century political leaders William Pitt, 1st Earl of Chatham (Pitt the Elder) and James Stanhope, 1st Earl Stanhope; politicians Jacob Rees-Mogg, Anthony Crosland, Jeremy Thorpe; Civil War Parliamentary general Henry Ireton; Flight Lieutenant Richard Hillary; Jay Gatsby, fictional alumnus from F. Scott-Fitzgerald's classic *The Great Gatsby*.

University College, High Street

Alternative names: The Master and Fellows of the College of the Great Hall of the University of Oxford (commonly called University College), Latin *Magister et Socij Collegij Magnae Aulae Universitatis Oxon;* colloquially Univ.

Founder: William of Durham, 1249.

College secrets: Although it claims to be the oldest of the colleges, no trace of the original medieval buildings remains above ground.

The Main Quad took forty years to complete, interrupted by the Civil War in the seventeenth century.

Logic Lane, off the High Street, is a private road owned by the college, which it bisects.

The statue of James II at the college – one of only two in the whole country – has no right hand. This absence remains a mystery. Whether it was broken by accident, by over-lusty pigeons or removed for obscure symbolic reasons, we may never know. Nor do we know what James may have held in that hand – if, indeed, it ever existed.

The Shelley Memorial is a specially constructed edifice, housing a statue of the poet Shelley by Edward Onslow Ford. The enclosing structure was designed by Basil Champneys. Shelley's daughter-in-law Lady Jane Shelley had originally commissioned a memorial to go in the Protestant cemetery in Rome, where the poet was buried. The memorial, however, was too large for the plot, and Jane scrabbled around to find an alternative. The rest is history and a million tourists a year.

The college boathouse was destroyed (along with a large archive) by arson in 1999. The new boathouse on the Thames was completed in 2007, and has been awarded a Royal Institute of British Architects (RIBA) prize.

University College celebrated its thousandth birthday in June 1872, and the Chancellor of the Exchequer led the toasts to founder King Alfred at the celebratory feast. Even at the time, this was a bit cheeky as it was widely accepted that the Alfred link, for all its plausibility and possibility, had no basis in written records. It is most probably an invention of the fourteenth century in an attempt to prove to Cambridge that Oxford was the older institution. So, the college will have to celebrate its thousandth birthday for a second time, in the year 2249.

Famous alumni and fellows: (Known as Univites) physician John Radcliffe, of hospitals fame; Beveridge Report author William Beveridge (Master of the College); UK Prime Ministers Clement Attlee, Harold Wilson (fellow); US president Bill Clinton; Australian Prime Minister Bob Hawke; Poet Laureate Andrew Motion; writer and academic C.S. Lewis; theatre director Ronald Eyre; Nobel Prize for Literature winner, Sir V.S. Naipaul; poet Stephen Spender; actors Michael York,

Warren Mitchel; radio DJ Paul Gambaccini; physicist Stephen Hawking; Rasputin murderer Prince Felix Yusupov; journalist/editor Richard Ingrams; writer/satirist Armando Iannucci.

Wadham College, Parks Road

Founder: Nicholas and Dorothy Wadham, wealthy land-owners, 1610.

College secrets: Dorothy Wadham did all the hard work after her husband's death. She fought legal battles to keep cash-hungry relations at bay, negotiated the college site and statutes, appointed the first warden, fellows, scholars and cook, and added more funds from her own resources. Everything was ready a mere four years after Nicholas's death. Dorothy kept tight control of college affairs until her own demise in 1618. During all this time, she never actually visited Oxford.

One of the monuments in the chapel features a pile of books. This commemorates Thomas Harris, one of the fellows appointed at the foundation by Dorothy Wadham. He died in 1614, aged twenty.

The college grounds include the Holywell Music Room, thought to be the oldest purpose-built concert hall in the world. It was designed by Thomas Camplin of St Edmund hall in July 1748. It contains a Donaldson organ built in 1790, but only installed in 1985 after restoration. It is the only surviving member of its musical tribe.

The Ferdowsi library was founded by funds from the Iranian monarchy in 1976. It is dedicated to Persian studies.

The extensive college gardens used to belong to an Augustinian priory, one of the Catholic institutions suppressed and stolen under the rule of King Henry VIII. The designers of the first gardens installed a rainbow maker and a talking statue. The gardens also contain remnants of Royalist earthworks from the Civil War.

Famous alumni and fellows: Oliver Cromwell's admiral of the fleet, Robert Blake; architects Christopher Wren, Thomas Graham Jackson; composer Sir Thomas Beecham; Poet Laureate Cecil Day-Lewis; MP Michael Foot; Archbishop of Canterbury Dr Rowan Williams; broadcaster and novelist Melvyn Bragg; novelists Monica Ali, Michael Kenyon; comic writer Alan Coren; New Zealand Premier William Fox; Prime Minister and president of Fiji Kamisese Mara; President of Pakistan Waseem Sajjad; clergyman and diarist Francis Kilvert; actors Tim McInnerny, Rosamund Pike, Jodhi May; poet and broadcaster Michael Rosen; libertine poet and satirist John Wilmot, 2nd Earl of Rochester.

Wolfson College, Linton Road

Alternative names: formerly Iffley College.

Founder: by committee, under the figureheads of Isaiah Berlin and the eponymous Sir Isaac Wolfson, 1966. college charter granted 1981.

College secrets: Iffley College opened in 1965, to provide a base for university academic staff who held no college fellowship. Sir Isaiah Berlin, fellow of All Souls, was the college's first president in 1966. The Wolfson Foundation (founded by philanthropist businessman Sir Isaac Wolfson) and the Ford Foundation came forward with money, and so the college adopted the Wolfson name. The first graduates were admitted in 1968, and the new buildings opened in 1974.

The college arms bear the image of the famous Norman decorated arch at Iffley Church, in honour of the institution's origins.

The college has an Isaiah Berlin Virtual Library, perpetuating the life and good works of the man.

Famous alumni and fellows: Quantum scientist Michele Mosca; novelist, art historian Iain Pears; UN International

Criminal Tribunals Prosecutor Karim Asad Ahmad Khan; civil justice authority Dame Hazel Genn; UK Green Party principal speaker Mike Woodin; novelist Amit Chaudhuri; historian Norman Davies; scientist, discoverer of the Epstein-Barr virus, Sir Anthony Epstein; computer scientist and developer of Quicksort Sir Tony Hoare; Indian historian Sumit Sarkar; author and screenwriter (including 1968's *Yellow Submarine*) Erich Wolf Segal; human geneticist Bryan Sykes; Nobel Prize-winning ethologist Niko Tinbergen.

Worcester College, Walton Street

Alternative names: Formerly Gloucester Hall.

Founder: Money left by Worcestershire landowner Sir Thomas Cookes, 1714. There were pre-Worcester foundations in the sixteenth and thirteenth centuries.

College secrets: Founded using the buildings of the suppressed Gloucester College, a Benedictine school. The market place and bus station area of Oxford, Gloucester Green, preserves the name of the old college.

Gloucester College was given to Robert King, the first Bishop of Oxford, after the Dissolution. He lived here until his new palace was ready in St Aldates. In 1560 Sir Thomas White, founder of St John's College, purchased the buildings, at which point it became known as Gloucester Hall.

The medieval cottages on the front quad only survive because money ran out during the eighteenth-century rebuild by Nicholas Hawksmoor and Sir George Clarke.

The interior of the chapel was redecorated by William Burges in 1864–66. Heavy on the pink, it has pews decorated with carved animals, and frescoes on the walls, including dodos (an animal with strong Oxford associations) and peacocks. John Everett Millais was pencilled in to design the stained glass windows, but Burges wasn't happy with them and gave Millias's fellow Pre-Raphaelite Henry Holiday the job instead.

Famous alumni and fellows: Author Richard Adams; film director and writer Alex Cox; TV producer and Doctor Who reviver Russell T. Davies; tycoon Rupert Murdoch; essayist Thomas *Confessions of an English Opium eater* de Quincey; businessman and supermarket magnate John Sainsbury (Baron Sainsbury of Preston Candover); Lord Justice of Appeal Sir Stephen Tomlinson; actress Emma *Harry Potter* Watson; fashion writer, novelist Victoria 'Plum' Sykes; politician and broadcaster Woodrow Lyle Wyatt, Baron Wyatt of Weeford; Grandmaster chess player Jonathan Simon 'Jon' Speelman; three-times Thai Prime Minster Mom Rajawongse Seni Pramoj.

Wycliffe Hall, Banbury Road

Founder: a group of evangelical churchmen, including Bishop of Liverpool J.C. Ryle, 1877. Became a permanent private hall in 1996.

College secrets: Named after radical theologian John Wycliffe, Master of Balliol Collage, who translated the Bible from Latin into English in 1382.

The majority of students at Wycliffe Hall are preparing for ordained ministry in the Church of England, or for other kinds of Christian ministry. The rest are studying Theology too. Wycliffe's stance is orthodox (High Church Anglican) rather than liberal – a more liberal approach to admissions in the 1960s was thought to have weakened the appeal of the institution.

Wycliffe is semi-independent of the university, governed by a non-university council whose members have to sign the college's Trust Deed, which safeguards its 'evangelical commitment to biblical theology and Christian mission' (as it says on their website).

The college's 'homely' look is due to the premises originally being designed in the 1860s as family houses. Its most prominent building at No. 52 Banbury Road was originally Holy Rood Convent.

Famous alumni and fellows: Politician, author and broadcaster Jonathan Aitken; the Revd Wilbert Vere *Thomas the Tank Engine* Awdry; former Archbishop of Canterbury Lord Coggan; and umpteen other theologians and main movers in the Anglican church, including Bishop of Liverpool the Rt Revd James Jones, author the Revd J.I. Packer, and former Bishop of Durham the Rt Revd N.T. Wright.

Chapter Three

Oxford
Celebrities

In writing of a city that has shaken hands with the Good, the Bad, the Ugly and most other members of Britain's Hall of Fame, it is hard to do justice to the tidal wave of celebrity that has crashed upon Oxford down the centuries. The following chronological trawl fishes out some of the more colourful scholars, scandals and secrets.

Roger Bacon

Roger Bacon (1214–94) was the preeminent thinker of his age. Legend insists that he once dressed himself as a common thatcher to meet a deputation from Cambridge University. The students from the 'Other Place' were so dismayed to find such a formidable intellect amongst the common populace that they ran back home, afraid of being put to shame by Oxford's genuine academics.

Amongst the man's many words of wisdom were 'half of science is asking the right questions' and the famous 'a little learning is a dangerous thing, but none at all is fatal.'

Roger Bacon theorised on a number of possible scientific advances, including motorised boats, pedal-powered flapping aeroplanes and carriages with engines (i.e. automobiles). He was so ahead of his time that he was accused of being a magician, and his famous study (which once decorated the southern end of Folly Bridge at Grandpont) was said to have been so cunningly constructed that it could be made to collapse on anyone who thought themselves cleverer than Bacon.

The study was actually built a century before Bacon's time, and it did indeed come tumbling down, demolished in 1779 during road-widening.

Edward of Woodstock

A portrait of Edward of Woodstock, more famously known as the Black Prince, hangs in the hall at Christ Church. Edward was the eldest son of King Edward III, embodiment of the patriotic English knight, and first Knight of the Garter in 1348. He was born in Woodstock, Oxfordshire, and had his main residence at Wallingford. His early death denied him the throne and his several illegitimate children somewhat undermined his image as the flower of chivalry.

Edward's badge, a fleur-de-lys on a black background, may be the origin of the 'black prince' tag. Legend also mentions black armour, and historical fact suggests the 'black' nickname may have been condemnatory, based on his brutal treatment of enemy soldiers during the fourteenth-century wars against France.

The Christ Church portrait was painted in the eighteenth century, and is known to be based not on images of the Prince himself, but on a handsome Oxford butcher's son.

Richard Foxe

Richard Foxe (1448–1528), Bishop of Winchester and founder of Corpus Christi College, played a vital role in Britain's Tudor and Stuart dynastic history. He was responsible for arranging two key royal marriages: Henry VIII to his elder brother's widow, Katherine of Aragon, and Henry's sister Margaret to the Scottish king James IV. This marriage laid the roots for her grandson James VI's claim to the English throne (as James I of England) after the death of the last Tudor, Elizabeth.

Desiderius Erasmus Roterodamus

Rushes used to play a vital role in urban life. The dried pith of the plant was used as a cheap form of light ('rush candles'), while the rest was used to cover floors in churches and other buildings. The philosopher and writer Erasmus (1466–1536), visiting Oxford in 1498, was unimpressed by this organic matting:

> The floors in general are laid with a white clay and are covered with rushes, occasionally removed, but so imperfectly that the bottom layer is left undisturbed, sometimes for twenty years, harbouring expectorations, vomitings, the leakage of dogs and men, ale-droppings, scraps of fish, and other abominations not fit to be mentioned. The island would be much more salubrious if the use of rushes were abandoned.

Rush lights were still being used in the nineteenth century, although rush flooring had finally disappeared from most places in the previous century.

Elizabeth I

The university did its best to encourage Elizabeth I's affections on her first visit to the city in 1566. It pasted odes to her beauty in Latin and Greek on the gates and walls of the colleges, each one apparently inspiring words of praise from the Queen. Young scholars flocked around her, exercising their bowing skills and quick wits. They managed to appeal to Elizabeth's playful side, some even receiving kisses and tips. According to John Cordy Jeaffreson in *Annals of Oxford*:

> She exhibited the hearty kindliness of an elder sister bent on making a riotous bevy of younger brothers enjoy a period of festivity. Arresting the lads as they marched before her with their caps in their hands, she gossiped with them about their homes, proved their quickness in capping verses, and, tickled into merriment by their frank answers to her reassuring speeches, laughingly told them that they were saucy boys, who needed much more whipping than they got from their tutors.

In Christ Church Hall things went awry when the performance of a new play – *Palamon and Arcyte*, by Richard Edwards – was marred by a collapsing stage, killing three and injuring five others. The corpses were removed, and the show went on (amidst much applause, we are told). Part two went ahead the following night without incident. The most memorable scene involved a fox hunt: a large group of people had been placed in the Great Quadrangle to impersonate the sounds of the hunt, and students inside the hall where the play was taking place joined in the make-believe by cheering the hounds. Elizabeth found all this very amusing, declaring, 'Oh excellent! Those boys in very truth are ready to leap out of the windows to follow the hounds!'

Playwright Edwards must have thought his theatrical and financial boat had come in. Unfortunately, he died a couple of months later.

The Queen revisited the city in 1592, and was apparently far less agreeable in her relative old age.

Christ Church Hall's interior.

Richard Haydock

In 1604 James I came to Oxford to investigate the sleepwalking preacher Richard Haydock, a fellow of New College. James's mission was to sniff out witchcraft, in the aftermath of his 1597 treatise on the subject, *Daemonologie*. Haydock had acquired national fame as a preacher, but the sermons only came to him in his sleep.

By day he could barely string two sentences together, due to a bad stammer. For this reason he had chosen to silently study medicine rather than preaching, his true vocation. But vocations have a way of catching up with you, and Haydock was wowing the faithful and the curious with what appeared to be divinely-inspired sleep-sermons.

It was a good wheeze, and a handy way of getting some extra money. But the fame that sermons brought him was nearly his downfall. If convicted of witchcraft, he was unlikely to survive for very long after the trial and so, sensing doom, he confessed. He wasn't really asleep, he said, but had carefully planned the sermons and learnt them by heart. It wasn't an easy ruse – his listeners would routinely pinch and slap him, to prove to themselves and other doubters that he was asleep – but Haydock always made it to the end of his speeches in spite of the audience intervention.

It was when faced with James in a private 'sleep preaching' session at New College that he caved in and confessed. He had wanted the attention, he said, because he felt himself 'a buried man at the university'. Speaking in bed with his eyes closed enabled him to escape his stammer, and he had started out innocently enough by writing sermons and then trying to recall them in his dreams.

James was unusually lenient, ordering Haydock to make his confession public, but leaving it at that. In gratitude, Haydock composed a treatise on dreams and dedicated it to the demon-hunting King.

Gilbert Sheldon

Sheldonian founder Gilbert Sheldon (1598–1677) was a graduate of Trinity College and fellow, and sometime Warden, of All Souls. He became Archbishop of Canterbury in 1663 and Chancellor of the university in 1667. But he was also a child of the permissive Restoration times. Diarist Samuel Pepys records a lusty and incestuous altercation between Sheldon and libertine Charles Sedley (1639–1701, Baronet, dramatist and politician):

> ...the Archbishop of Canterbury, that now is, do keep a wench, and that he is as very a wencher as can be... it is a thing publicly known that Sir Charles Sedley had got away one of the Archbishop's wenches from him, and the Archbishop sent to him to let him know that she was his kinswoman, and did wonder that he would offer any dishonour to one related to him. To which Sir Charles Sedley is said to answer: 'A pox take his Grace! pray tell his Grace that I believe he finds himself too old, and is afraid that I should outdo him among his girls, and spoil his trade.' But he makes no more of doubt to say that the Archbishop is a wencher, and known to be so, which is one of the most astonishing things that I have heard of.

William Davenant

William Davenant claimed that he was the illegitimate son of William Shakespeare. The bard is thought to have regularly lodged in Oxford en route from Stratford to London, and Davenant was happy to concur with a piece of handy folklore regarding Shakespeare's fondness for Jane Shepherd Davenant, the wife of Oxford Mayor and wine merchant John Davenant. The latter kept the Bull Inn, later called the Crown Inn (not the current Crown Inn, but the still-standing building at No. 3 Cornmarket – the eighteenth-century exterior masks its sixteenth-century origins).

Shakespeare is said to have been godfather to baby William at St Martin's, Carfax, in 1606, but gossip and folklore soon sniffed out a much more exciting story. Perhaps Jane was seeking respite from her downbeat husband: according to seventeenth-century historian Anthony Wood, Davenant senior 'was a very grave and discreet citizen (yet an admirer of plays and play-makers, especially Shakespeare, who frequented his house in his journeys between Warwickshire and London), was of a melancholic disposition, and was seldom or never known to laugh.'

Archbishop Laud

William Laud, Archbishop of Canterbury and Chancellor of Oxford University, entered St John's College as a student in 1590, and was college president in 1611. An influential man caught in turbulent times, Laud was an anti-Puritan supporter of Charles I and executed for his unflinching faith in High Church teachings. During his tenure of the Chancellorship of Oxford University Laud bolstered the academic clout of the university, increasing the numbers of students, good teachers and serviceable buildings.

One of the Archbishop's supposed crimes on his slow road to execution under the Puritans was 'repairing cruci-fixes.' He was also condemned for reinstating the image of the Virgin Mary over the door of St Mary's on the High Street. A blabbermouth Puritan Alderman called Nixon provided damning evidence, declaring that he had seen a man 'bowing to the scandalous image'.

Parliament accused Laud of treason in 1640, and in 1641 he was imprisoned in the Tower of London. Despite a royal pardon, he was condemned and beheaded at Tower Hill on 10 January 1645. Originally buried in London, he was reinterred beneath the altar in the chapel at St John's. His ghost is sometimes seen walking a few inches above the ground, and has even been known to bowl its head across the floor.

John Clavell

I that have robb'd so oft, am now bid stand,
Death, and the Law assault me, and demand
My life, and meanes; I never us'd men so,
But having ta'ne their money, let them goe.

John Clavell wrote the first draft of this poem, *A Recantation of an Ill Led Life* from prison, under sentence of death. He sent it to King James, in hope of a royal pardon.

Clavell studied at Brasenose between 1619 and 1621, but never took his degree. Instead, he readied himself for a life of crime. In April 1621 he narrowly avoided imprisonment after stealing some of the college's silver, but mounting debts persuaded him that robbery was the most practical option. His stint as highwayman lasted from 1624 and 1626, after which he was captured and reduced to penning indifferent verses from his cell.

Surprisingly, Clavell's poem appealed to James's sense of rhyme and reason, and the death penalty was lifted. The reformed highwayman spent two years in prison; then, on the strength of his fame, he attempted to break into the theatrical trade with the play *The Soddered Citizen*. The King's Company (to which Shakespeare had once belonged) performed it in the early 1630s, but it was not well received. Ever pragmatic, Clavell made another career switch, working as a lawyer and physician in Ireland.

His play was assumed to be lost forever. But in 1932, 300 years after its only performance, a manuscript was discovered, bearing the author's signature. *A Soddered Citizen* revival is yet to be staged.

William Harvey

William Harvey, the man who untangled the mysteries of blood circulation, was made Warden of Merton
College in 1645, during the English Civil War. Charles I
had titled him Doctor of Physic three years earlier.
Merton was one of the few Parliamentarian-supporting
parts of the university, hence the rapid promotion of
Royalist Harvey when the king commandeered the city.
The Warden post did not last long: the Surrender of
Oxford was signed a few months after his installation
and Harvey retired, aged sixty-eight. He died in 1657,
having refused to return to what he called 'the faithless
sea' of academic medical life. Appropriately enough,
he died of a blood circulation problem: a rupture of a
cerebral artery (brain haemorrhage) brought about by
years of gout-inflicted damage.

Anthony Wood

Anthony Wood (1632–95) was a historian whose colour-
less prose is invaluable as a record of the seventeenth
century (he was a child evacuee in the Civil War, fleeing
to Thame), and also as an in-depth trawl through the
minutiae of what went before in the city of Oxford.
A modest memorial plaque can be seen in Merton
Chapel and his former home, the Postmasters' Hall, is
still standing on Merton Street. As nineteenth-century
historian Andrew Lang noted, 'No one who cares for
the past of the university should think without pity and
friendliness of this lonely scholar, who in his lifetime was
unpitied and unbefriended'.

Wood fell out with almost everyone he knew, including Dick Peers, the man who translated Wood's *Athenae
Oxonienses: an Exact History of all the Writers and Bishops*

Postmasters' Hall, Merton Street. (Photograph by Jan Sullivan)

who have had their Education in the University of Oxford from 1500 to 1690 (originally published in two volumes, 1691–92). Peers had been commissioned by Dean Fell of Christ Church, and he was told to correct any passages in which Wood's religious and political inclinations differed from those of Fell. Wood was judged a Catholic and Jacobite sympathiser, and Fell most certainly wasn't.

The resulting alterations in the Latin text infuriated Wood. He had frequent violent fall-outs with the translator, one at a tavern on the High Street, and one at the printing house in the Sheldonian Theatre. Peers, according to contemporary reports, 'always cometh off with a bloody nose or a black eye' and eventually hid himself away to avoid bumping into his pugilistic foe. The tables were turned when Peers became a University Proctor, and now it was Wood who went into hiding, fearing that Peers might seek revenge for his pummelling.

Of the many institutions in the city, Wood reserved the highest praise for Magdalen College, 'the most noble and rich structure in the learned world' with its water walks as 'delectable as the banks of Eurotas, where Apollo himself was wont to walk.'

In November 1695 a man called Wylde stumbled upon the sixty-three-year-old Wood digging in Merton Chapel. The historian explained that he was digging his own grave. He was ill, and suspected that he did not have long to live. He was keen to make sure that his final resting place was the right dimensions, and in exactly the right place, 'close to the wall, next to the north door.' He's still lying there, hopefully eternally satisfied with his handiwork.

The Earl of Clarendon

Edward Hyde, 1st Earl of Clarendon (1609–74), was Chancellor of the university between 1660 and 1667. He was the author of *The History of the Great Rebellio*n, the first history of the English Civil War, and the proceeds from this book went towards the foundation of the Clarendon Building (1711–15). This was built to house the University Press (which had previously operated from the basement of the Sheldonian Theatre, so the presses had to be silent if any ceremony or concert was taking place). The Press moved to new premises on Walton Street a hundred years later and the Clarendon currently serves as offices for the Bodleian Library.

Hyde's money went even further: his trustees paid £10,000 for the building of the Clarendon Laboratory on Parks Road, which opened in 1872. It is the oldest purpose-built physics laboratory in England, currently part of the university's Earth Sciences Faculty.

Hyde was the grandfather of two Stuart Queens, Mary II and Anne. His daughter Anne was married to the ill-fated

James II. Hyde himself was a graduate of Magdalen Hall, now known as Hertford College. His portrait hangs in the college hall.

Samuel Johnson

Pembroke College Master John Ratcliffe (who took up the post in 1738) earned the wrath of Doctor Samuel Johnson in 1754, after refusing to purchase the great man's new Dictionary. He had given Johnson a cold reception during the writer's supposedly triumphant return to his old Oxford College. Johnson fumed, 'There lives a man, who lives by the renowns of literature, and will not move a finger to support it.' Johnson's desk can be seen in Broadgates Hall (a part of Pembroke retaining the institution's pre-college name).

Johnson had struggled with pride and poverty during his abortive studies at Pembroke. When a friend left a pair of new shoes at his door, having noted the holes in his old ones, Johnson flung them away in indignation. In general he was remembered as 'a gay frolicsome fellow' but in later years Johnson recalled little but the poverty. 'Ah, Sir, I was mad and violent,' he confessed. 'It was bitterness they mistook for frolic. I was miserably poor and thought to fight my way by my literature and my wit, so I disregarded all power and authority.'

When Johnson looked back on his career in later life he was slightly rueful concerning his drinking habits, 'I did not leave off drinking wine because I could not bear it. I have drunk off three bottles of port without being the worse of it. University College has witnessed this.'

Kettell Hall, the building now known as No. 54 Broad Street next to Blackwells book shop, was a favourite haunt of Johnson in his post-university days. It was where his friend, historian and Poet Laureate Thomas Warton lived.

John Radcliffe

John Radcliffe did not live to see Oxford's Radcliffe Camera. It was funded with money bequeathed by him in 1714 to house a medical library (Radcliffe being the physician who opened the city's first infirmary, and after whom

The Radcliffe Camera.

the modern John Radcliffe hospital is named). The Camera was built by James Gibbs between 1737 and 1749 after he beat Nicholas Hawksmoor for the honour.

Described by historian Goldwin Smith as a 'Court physician and despot of the profession', Radcliffe told gouty William III, 'I wouldn't have His Majesty's legs for all His three kingdoms.' On another occasion he took offence at a patient's inability to pay for his services, and made an angry outburst predicting the poor man's imminent death. The man did indeed die soon after – out of sheer terror, it was said.

William Blackstone

William Blackstone (1723–1780) was an academic and writer whose commentaries on law became the foundation stone for modern legal thinking in Britain and the USA. He was a student at Pembroke, and an important figure at All Souls in later days. Contemporaries described him as combining mental irritability with physical sloth, and he is said to have written his cornerstone work, *Commentaries on the Laws of England*, with a bottle of port in front of him. Amongst his more universal innovations was the introduction into college of the corkscrew and the well-stocked college wine cellar.

James Sadler

The second balloonist, and the first Englishman, to take off from England was James Sadler. Inspired by the ascent of Vincent Lunardi at Moorfields in London less than a month previously, on 4 October 1784 Sadler took off from the north side of Oxford's Christ Church Meadow, touching down 6 miles later at Woodeaton. He had reached a maximum height of 1,100m (3,600ft) during the journey.

In the following year he made it as far as Aylesbury. He launched himself airwards again on the 12th, when a huge throng turned out to witness the event. After ditching the balloon somewhere beyond Thame, Sadler returned to Oxford, and was accosted by a wildly enthusiastic crowd. 'The populace seized the chaise at the entrance of the town, took off the horses, dragged the carriage

St Peter-in-the-East. (Photograph by Jan Sullivan)

through several of the principal streets of this city, and were not content till they had compelled the inhabitants to illuminate their houses.'

Sadler's third ride in the balloon took place in May 1785, and upon landing (near Pontefract in Yorkshire, having taken off from a garden on what was later called Balloon Street in Manchester) he was dragged for 2 miles by the brake-free balloon. In spite of this he remained a regular aeronaut, narrowly escaping drowning on a couple of occasions when his vehicle plunged into water. It was the death of his younger son Windham, in a ballooning accident in 1824, that finally deflated his spirits. He died in 1828, aged seventy-five. There is a plaque in the former St Peter-in-the-East Church (now part of St Edmund Hall), and a gravestone in the adjoining cemetery. There is also a plaque marking that first ascent, on Dead Man's Walk in Christ Church Meadow.

Nell Batchelor

Nell Batchelor was a pie seller in the mid-eighteenth century. An anonymous wit gave her the following epitaph:

Here under the dust
Is the mouldering crust
Of Eleanor Batchelor shoven,
Well versed in the art
Of pie, custard and tart
And the lucrative skill of the oven.
When she'd lived long enough
She made her last puff,
A puff by her husband much praised;
Now here she doth lie
And makes a dirt pie
In the hope that her crust may be raised.

Posterity recalls a handful of other Oxford street sellers: Dicky Dunker the cake man, whose chief customers were the inhabitants of Magdalen College; Mother Smith, with her street-cry of 'Any cakes and rolls, muffins and crumpets!'; Tippety Ward selling cakes 'all sugar and brandy!'; and 'Mother Goose' who sold bouquets of flowers at the city's coach stops and boasted the Prince Regent as one of her customers (he once tossed her a guinea at the Lamb and Flag on St Giles). 'Jack the Matchman', meanwhile, served with General Wolfe, who died after the British victory at the Battle of Quebec in 1759. Jack is immortalised in Benjamin West's 1770 painting The Death of General Wolfe, leaning on his musket and gazing at the dying General. Such fame as it was brought no financial rewards: Jack ended his days selling the old-fashioned, rather unpredictable, potassium and sulphur matches that existed before modern 'friction' matches were invented in 1826.

William Turner

One of Oxfordshire's most celebrated artists is William Turner (1789–1862), often dubbed 'Turner of Oxford' to differentiate him from the more famous, and not entirely dissimilar, J.M.W. Turner. He was born in the county at Black Bourton, lived for many years at the Manor House in Shipton-on-Cherwell, and ended his days on St John's Street in Oxford (commemorated by a blue plaque). He was buried in Holy Cross churchyard at Shipton, having designed the new building during the Victorian Gothic Revival onslaught. The 'of Oxford' tag is highly apt, as his most celebrated works involve, or are informed by, views and details of the landscape around the city.

Walter Landor

Walter Savage Landor (1775–1864) was an under-graduate at Trinity College, though he never finished his degree. The poet Robert Southey explained that Landor was not forced to leave the university for his extreme Jacobin (pro-French Revolution) views, but 'for shooting at one of the Fellows through a window.' The target was one Mr Leeds, a Tory, whose excessive partying, its accompanying noise and unpleasant political odour was sufficient to give Landor the excuse to reach for his gun.

Landor's defence was not very effective:

> I should have blushed to have had any conversation with them... But my gun was lying on a table in the room, and I had, in a back closet, some little shot. I proposed, as they had closed the casements, and as the shutters were on the outside, to fire a volley. It was thought a good trick, and accordingly I went into my bedroom and fired.

Percy Bysshe Shelley

Percy Bysshe Shelley (1792–1822) maintained an avid interest in chemistry, and he went to Oxford with the belief that science afforded greater leisure and instruc-tion than art. This belief did not last long. In his first week he attended a lecture on mineralogy, but left before the end. According to his biographer T.J. Hogg, he 'burst into my room, threw down his cap, and as he stood shivering and chafing his hands over the fire, declared how much he had been disappointed in the lecture. Few persons attended; it was dull and languid, and he resolved never to go to another.' Shelley's comment was, 'I stole away, for it was so stupid, and I was so cold that my teeth chat-tered.' Here he betrayed his artistic nature, declaring,

'Stones, stones, stones, nothing but stones! And so drily. It was wonderfully tiresome, and stones are not interesting things in themselves!'

In spite of this, the highly precocious and philanthropic Shelley remained convinced that science, in areas such as flight (the first balloons having captured the world's imagination), the harnessing of electricity (through 'electrical kites' tapping into thunderstorms) and the enrichment of poor soil, would transform the world.

The evidence of his chemical substance abuse was visible in his room and about his person. Hogg says his hands, clothes, books, carpet and furniture were all stained and burnt by his endeavours. In the middle of the room there was a large hole in the floorboards caused by a 'spontaneous ignition' when one of the crucibles spilled its contents. The ever-pacing Shelley would continually catch his foot in the hole and stumble. The cups and crockery of his room were roped in to hold his raw materials and experiments. Hogg, fearing that Shelley would one day poison himself and/or his guests, recalls that he was about to pour tea when he noticed a half-dissolved coin in one of the teacups, evidence of an experiment with acids. Shelley sympathised, having ingested arsenic as a younger man in the aftermath of some such mad experiment, and having never entirely recovered his health as a result.

At one point Shelley was learning to fire pistols, and took to walking through Oxford armed. His carelessness in waving the weapon around horrified poor Hogg, who nonetheless managed to coach his friend in the accurate use of firearms.

Shotover Hill was a favourite resort of Shelley's, and he was often seen standing by an old quarry lake there, where:

he would linger until dusk, gazing in silence on the water, repeating verses aloud or earnestly discussing themes that had no connection with surrounding objects. Sometimes he would raise a stone as large as he could lift, deliberately throw it into the water as far as his strength enabled him, then he would loudly exult at the splash.

He also loved skimming flat stones across the lake, and launching paper boats. It was said that he once found himself in Kensington Gardens with no paper other than a bank-post bill for fifty pounds. Unable to resist, he transformed the note into a boat, and waited at the far side of the lake for the vessel to land.

Beautiful as his verse may be, Shelley's spoken voice did not match. 'There was one physical blemish that threatened to neutralise all his excellence,' declares his biographer Hogg. '[His voice] was excruciating. It was intolerably shrill, harsh and discordant; it excoriated the ears.'

Shelley, to his horror, was expelled from University College after writing a tract entitled *The Necessity of Atheism*. In spite of this, the poet has a much revered monument, The Shelley Memorial, by Henry Onslow Ford, at University College (although visitors need permission to view it). Carved in Connemara marble, Shelley is depicted drowned and naked, a reference to his death at the age of thirty from drowning in stormy seas in Italy. He had been sailing from Livorno to Lerici in his schooner the *Don Juan*. He was cremated on a funeral pyre on the beach near Viareggio. Now hailed as one of the all-time greats, at the time of his death not everyone waxed lyrical. The Tory newspaper *The Courier* reported, 'Shelley, the writer of some infidel poetry, has been drowned, now he knows whether there is God or no.'

Beau Brummell

George Bryan 'Beau' Brummell was a renowned eighteenth-century dandy. He was the chief fashion guru of his day, astounding posh society not just with his clothes, but with his eccentric habit of cleaning his teeth and bathing – every day. His lounge-lizard approach to life is said to have been inspired by his time at Oriel College. As an under-graduate in 1793 he competed for the Newdigate Prize (awarded for the best verse), but lost. He was so affronted at not winning that he vowed never to exert himself again, and poured disdain on books and academia.

Brummell's prominent nose was the result of a kick from a horse during the dandy's stint in the 10th Dragoons.

Martin and Eliza Routh

Eliza Routh was the wife of the eccentric Dr Martin Routh, president of Magdalen College from 1791 to 1854. Riding her donkey through the streets of the city, Eliza presented a memorable spectacle, as recalled by William Tuckwell in his 1900 book *Reminiscences of Oxford*:

> ...between 'her dear man', as she called [Routh], and herself – 'that crathy old woman', as he occasionally called her – were nearly forty years. But she had become rapidly and prematurely old: with strongly marked features, a large moustache, and a profusion of grey hair, she paraded the streets, a spectral figure, in a little chaise drawn by a donkey and attended by a hunchback lad named Cox. 'Woman,' her husband would say to her, when from the luncheon table he saw Cox leading the donkey carriage round, 'Woman, the ass is at the door.'

This startling lady's husband was known as the Venerable Routh. He was still sporting eighteenth-century fashions in the 1850s, including the otherwise long-gone periwig. He remembered seeing Dr Samuel Johnson lost in thought on the High Street and he remained Magdalen's president until he died, close to his hundredth birthday. Tuckwell wrote of him:

> The wig, with trencher cap insecurely poised above it, the long cassock, ample gown, shorts and buckled shoes; the bent form, pale venerable face, enormous pendent eyebrows, generic to antique portraits in Bodleian gallery of college halls, were here to be seen alive.

William Buckland

William Buckland (1784–1856) was Oxford's first lecturer in Geology, and he and his son Frank were two of the most colourful characters ever produced by the university. Both kept houses that doubled as menageries, and their knowledge of all things animal – including how edible the various species were – was enormous. Buckland senior used to claim that he had eaten his way through the whole of animal creation: at first he thought the mole was the nastiest thing he had ever tasted, but later decided that blue-bottles were worse.

William Tuckwell, writing about the Bucklands, recalls that 'Frank used to tell of their visit ... to a foreign cathedral, where was exhibited a martyr's blood-dark spots on the pavement ever fresh and ineradicable. The professor dropped on the pavement and touched the stain with his tongue. "I can tell you what it is; it is bat's urine!"'

This was not his only episode of myth-debunking. During a visit to the shrine of St Rosalia in Palermo, Sicily, he asked to see the famous bones of the Saint. '[The shrine] was opened by the priests, and the relics of the saint were shown..."They are the bones of a goat," he cried out, "not of a woman"; and the sanctuary doors were abruptly closed.'

This original Mad Professor died on 24 August 1856, aged seventy-three, and is buried in Islip at a spot pre-chosen by him in the village churchyard. Frank Buckland died in 1880.

Thomas Huxley and Samuel Wilberforce

When Charles Darwin first published his evolutionary theory, many men, including eminent biologist Thomas Huxley, kicked themselves for not getting there first. It was, said Huxley, one of those things which seems blindingly obvious once it has been explained, the evidence, in the form of farm animals, dog breeds, fancy pigeons, etc., having been there for centuries.

Not everyone was open to the revolutionary implications of Darwin's work, though. A celebrated evolution-versus-creation debate took place in 1860, led by Thomas Huxley and Samuel Wilberforce, Bishop of Oxford. It was twelve months after the appearance of Darwin's *On the Origin of Species*, and Huxley (aka Darwin's Bulldog, the Richard Dawkins of his day) had visited the almost-completed university museum to attend a meeting of the British Association. The museum had been established as a repository of the city's various natural history collections, which at that time were housed not just at the Ashmolean but in some of the colleges too.

Huxley had intended to leave before the debate, but was goaded into taking a leading part. Wilberforce expressed his dismay at the thought that 'a venerable ape' might be his ancestor, asking Huxley whether it was through his grandfather or grandmother that he claimed such descent. To which the vehement Huxley replied:

> If I am asked whether I would choose to be descended from the poor animal of low intelligence and stooping gait, who grins and chatters as we pass, or from a man, endowed with great ability and splendid position, who should use these gifts to discredit and crush humble seekers after truth, I hesitate what answer to make.

There is a wall plaque in the museum pointing out the room in which this confrontation took place, and in 2010 a memorial stone was unveiled on the museum's lawn to mark the debate's 150th anniversary. There are also various ape-related relics in the edifice's glass cases.

William Spooner

William Archibald Spooner (1844–1930) was famous for metathesis, the accidental consonant-swapping ever afterwards known as Spoonerisms. The man himself (who may have blamed his poor eyesight – a symptom of his albinism – for certain misread passages) denied uttering almost all the tips of the slung credited to him, with the exception of 'cinquering Kongs their titles take' (the title of a hymn), and 'the weight of rages will press hard upon the employer.' Folklore, however, credits him with several classics, including:

The Lord is a shoving leopard (loving shepherd)

He was killed by a blushing crow (crushing blow)

Let us glaze our rasses to the queer old dean (raise our glasses/dear old Queen). The phrase was pronounced 'glaze our arses' for added hilarity.

We'll have the hags flung out (flags hung out)

Which of us has not felt in his heart a half-warmed fish? (half-formed wish)

A well-boiled icicle (well-oiled bicycle)

And the classic: You have hissed all my mystery lectures, and were caught fighting a liar in the quad. Having tasted two worms, you will leave by the next town drain!

It was not just consonants, but entire concepts that got muddled. He once referred to a woman whose husband 'was eaten by missionaries'. Crowds used to turn out to hear his lectures – not, as he admonished them, to hear the content, but to listen out for spoonerisms.

Lewis Carroll

Lewis Carroll, or Charles Dodgson as he was more properly known to his colleagues and students at Christ Church, was famous for his wildly imaginative and humorous writings. But in the flesh he was often a disappointment to his many fans. William Tuckwell reminisced:

> Of course, he was one of the sights of Oxford: strangers, lady strangers especially, begged their lionising friends to point out Mr Dodgson, and were disappointed when they saw the homely figure and the grave, repellent face. Except to little girls, he was not an alluring personage. Austere, shy, precise, absorbed in mathematical reverie, watchfully tenacious of his dignity, stiffly conservative in political, theological, social theory, his life mapped out in squares like Alice's landscape, he struck discords in the frank harmonious camaraderie of college life. The irreconcilable dualism of his exceptional nature, incongruous blend of extravagant frolic with self-conscious puritan repression, is interesting as a psychological study now that he is gone, but cut him off while living from all except the 'little misses' who were his chosen associates.

Edward Pusey and John Henry Newman

Keble College founder Edward Pusey is the only college founder to be honoured with a church feast day (i.e. like a saint). The Episcopal Church in the USA venerates him on 18 September. Pusey's contemporary, the equally prominent and influential Tractarian John Henry Newman, became a saint of the Catholic Church in 2010, with a feast day on 19 September.

C.S. Lewis

Oxford professor and Narnia creator Clive Staples Lewis was known as Jack to his friends and family. At the age of four he had lost his pet dog Jacksie in a road accident, and insisted on adopting the animal's name as his own. The love of animals stayed with him, and he claimed that his earliest literary and creative influences were the anthropomorphic creations of Beatrix Potter.

Graduating at University College Oxford, Lewis taught at Magdalen College from 1925–54 before transferring to Cambridge. His biggest legacy in modern Oxford is the C.S. Lewis Nature Reserve at Risinghurst, formerly part of the grounds of his house The Kilns, which is now a private residence with a blue plaque to the famous scholar-author. But on the international stage he is known primarily for his *Narnia* books, and his many writings on Christianity (having converted from atheism, largely under the influence of the devout J.R.R. Tolkien). Lewis is also famous for his relationship with fatally ill American writer Joy Gresham in his late fifties, a story immortalised in the 1993 movie *Shadowlands*, directed by Richard Attenborough.

William Morris

William Morris, owner of Morris Motors and creator of 'affordable motoring', was born in 1877, in a terraced house in Cowley near Oxford. These Everyman beginnings never entirely left him, and he continued to be a philanthropic benefactor and instigator, even when untold wealth had removed him several social strata from his modest beginnings. He was, by all accounts, neither warm nor charismatic, just endlessly practical.

His business breakthrough came at the age of sixteen with a bicycle repair business in the shed at the bottom of the family garden. Having shifted from bikes to cars, he designed his first commercial model, the Morris Oxford (aka the Bullnose Morris), in 1912, moving the workshop to a disused military training college in Cowley soon after. The 'affordable motoring' concept literally changed the nature of Britain's roads, bringing motor vehicles within reach of a broad cross-section of the population.

During the First World War, the Cowley works produced munitions, just as it was to manufacture Spitfires and Tiger Moths in the Second bout, and Morris's star was firmly in the firmament. He was knighted in 1929, and later moved to Nuffield Place near Henley-on-Thames, becoming Lord Nuffield in 1934.

By 1937 Morris Motors Ltd was the largest motor manufacturer in Europe. The inflow of money into the Nuffield coffers was unstoppable. Morris founded Nuffield College in this year, even though it was not completed until 1960 due to building 'rationing' during the post-war rearmament drive. In 1943 the Nuffield Foundation was founded with a kick-start of £10 million. Indeed, it is said that William Morris gave away the equivalent in today's money of £11 billion. He died in 1963.

J.R.R. Tolkien

J.R.R. Tolkien was a pipe-smoking university academic who had no interest in fame and celebrity, and yet, in 2009, was judged the highest earning dead writer in the world, on account of book sales and other Middle Earth merchandise and movie-related goods.

In life Tolkien was Rawlinson and Bosworth Professor of Anglo-Saxon at Oxford University from 1925 to 1945, and Merton Professor of English Language and Literature from then until 1959, with earlier stints writing for *The Oxford English Dictionary*. A student of Exeter College, as a

Professor he was based first at Pembroke and then at Merton. Oxford currently has a J.R.R. Tolkien Professor of English Literature and Language post in memory of the man's work and influence.

Tolkien is buried with his wife Edith in the cemetery at Wolvercote in north Oxford, and there are blue plaques on his one-time residences at No. 76 Sandfield Road and No. 20 Northmoor Road in suburban Oxford. His favourite city watering hole, the Eagle and Child on St Giles, is a busy beery shrine for pilgrims of Tolkien and his close friend C.S. Lewis.

The ultimately melancholy tone of Tolkien's fictional works – his Legendarium, as he called it – owes its hue to the atmosphere surrounding the mythology's formation. He began writing *The Book of Lost Tales*, the first inroads into the Middle Earth-related universe, whilst recovering from illness that resulted from his presence at the Battle of the Somme in 1916.

The tweedy, waist-coated, pipe-smoking ghost of the Professor is occasionally spotted in the precincts of Merton College. Later occupants of his study have reported the smell of tobacco, as if its pipe-loving occupant had vacated the premises moments before.

Richard Hillary and Leonard Cheshire

The Oxford University Air Squadron was the source of many fighters in the Battle of Britain, including Spitfire ace Richard Hillary who was shot down twice in 1939 after taking down several enemy planes. Rising again from extensive plastic surgery – an area pioneered at Oxford – he was shot down for the last time in 1943.

The most famous member of the Squadron was Group Captain Leonard Cheshire. Awarded the Victoria Cross, it was his 103rd mission – as the official British observer of the nuclear bombing of Nagasaki – that changed his life. From then on he poured his money and efforts into charitable works, the most lasting being the health and welfare charity the Leonard Cheshire Foundation (called Leonard Cheshire Disability since 2007).

Vera Brittain

Writer Vera Brittain (1893–1970), alumnus of Somerville College, lost most of her loved ones in the First World War, including her fiancé and brother. She worked as a nursing auxiliary, studied in Oxford again after the war, and became a successful writer and speaker. Her fame as a 'principled pacifist' and her influential voice on the international stage is underlined beautifully by her inclusion in Hitler's notorious 'Black Book', which named 2,000 people to be immediately arrested in Britain after the Germans invaded.

James Fulbright

Senator James William Fulbright (1905–95) founded the Fulbright Scholarships, reflecting his interest in international relations and academic international exchange programmes. He was a Rhodes Scholar at Pembroke College in the 1920s, and earned wonderfully evocative praise from the college's master, Ronald McCallum, in 1963. Speaking to a newspaper, McCallum stated 'Fulbright is responsible for the greatest movement of scholars across the face of the earth since the fall of Constantinople in 1453.'

Fulbright was a prime mover in the establishment of the United Nations, and was a vocal opponent of some of America's worst decisions, including McCarthyism and the Vietnam War.

Chapter Four

Oxford
Buildings

A peep through the keyholes of the iconic buildings that have
defined the city from the twelfth to the twenty-first century.

Beaumont, Oxford's royal palace

Beaumont Palace was built in 1130 by King Henry I as
his *nova aula* (new hall), just beyond the north gate of
Oxford. It was conveniently close to the Woodstock Royal
Hunting Lodge further north in the county. Kings Henry II,
Richard I and John were all born here.

Edward I (reigned
1272-1307) gave the Palace
to Italian lawyer, university
lecturer and royal diplomat
Francesco Accorsi in 1275.
In 1318 Edward's successor
Edward II gave it to God, in
the form of Carmelite Friars,
in thanks for his survival at
the Battle of Bannockburn
in 1314. This religious incarnation lasted until the 1530s
when Henry VIII dissolved
the Palace/Friary, along with

King Henry II.

all other Catholic establishments. Beaumont was dismantled and its stones were used in the construction of Oxford
Colleges Christ Church and St John's. The last remnants of
the old Oxford Palace were levelled in 1829 when modern
Beaumont Street was laid across this corner of the city. Its
site is marked with a plaque.

City Walls

Oxford's city walls enclosed approximately 115 urban
acres. They had an internal walkway (like the surviving wall walks at places such as Chester and York),
with a 2-mile circumference. The four roads that led
from the four city gates still form the centre of Oxford,
meeting at the crossroads of Carfax (the word being a
Chinese-whispered leap from Latin *Quadrifurcus*, a place
where four roads meet).

The best surviving section of the thirteenth-century city
walls (an upgrade of the original wooden ramparts) can
be seen in the grounds of New College, looking amazingly
pristine. There are other good chunks at St Edmund's
Hall, Corpus Christi and Christ Church Colleges, and one
or two other visible stretches. Strictly speaking these are
town walls, rather than city walls, as Oxford only became
a city when the See of Oxford was created in 1542 (a 'see'
is a religious area – prior to 1542 Oxford had belonged to
the enormous See of Lincoln).

From Priory to College

Christ Church College symbolises the political and social
upheavals of the early sixteenth century. It was originally
founded by King Henry VIII's first henchman, Cardinal
Thomas Wolsey. A great patron of learning, Wolsey had
taken his BA at Magdalen in 1486, aged fifteen. He also

had an eye for financial profit, and scurrilous legend suggests that he misappropriated funds during the money-raising that accompanied the construction of Magdalen's bell tower (Wolsey being college Bursar at the time).

To finance the new foundation, he made a pre-emptive strike on the country's monasteries (the Dissolution still being several years away). In 1522 he managed to get both king and Pope to sanction the closure of St Frideswide's Priory in Oxford. In an act of hubris worthy of Shakespearian tragedy, the confiscated land and buildings became Cardinal's College in 1525, the Priory church, in truncated form, becoming the college chapel.

But King Henry then set his heart on Anne Boleyn and separation from the Roman church, and the Cardinal's downfall was set in motion. Henry seized the college with the intention of closing it, but in 1532, with Wolsey dead, it was refounded as King Henry VIII's College.

The final piece of the puzzle was slotted into place in 1546 when the Anglican See of Oxford was established, with its base at the old Priory church. To mark the occasion, and to reflect the unique amalgamation of secular college and Anglican Cathedral, the institution was given yet another foundation, this time as Christ Church College.

The Reinvention of Oxford Castle

Empress Matilda, denied the crown of England by her cousin and rival King Stephen during the twelfth-century Anarchy (see p. 21), was imprisoned at Oxford Castle. She has haunted it ever since, and, according to less-than-scientific statistics, was the most frequently identified ghost in Britain between 2007–09, notching up thirty-two manifestations. The only thing to conclude is that Matilda's ghost must be unmistakable, otherwise how on earth (or heaven or hell) would we know which apparition we were looking at?

Oxford Castle.

St George's Tower at Oxford Castle.

Queen Matilda.

The eleventh-century Norman tower of St George at Oxford Castle gained a macabre modern face in the nineteenth century when the New Drop was installed here. Here condemned criminals would stand, ropes around their necks, and breathe their last before the trapdoor opened. It was slightly more humane than the older method of letting them swing by the neck until suffocated, as the drop was guaranteed to snap necks swiftly.

The castle site was owned by Christ Church College until 1785, when the city magistrates purchased it. The site had been used as a prison since the civil wars of the previous century and, like most gaols of the day, it was mainly a place to hold prisoners pending trial. Their fate after this was usually execution or transportation, but after the American War of Independence the usual port of call for transportees, Virginia, was suddenly out of bounds. Prisons could barely soak up the excess inmates and Oxford's was certainly in a sorry state, with overcrowding from human, rodent and invertebrate populations, and all their attendant disease.

After the prison closed in 1996 the site became derelict, but reopened as a visitor attraction in 2007, featuring mock wardens, grisly ghost stories, and a couple of bistros. It hosts various markets and events throughout the year, with its Christmas German-style fair being the most popular.

The Bocardo

This eleventh-century structure was the original city gaol, next to St Michael's Church at the George Street end of Cornmarket. Its famous occupants include the Oxford Martyrs Cranmer, Ridley and Latimer (see p. 27), although its mainstream prisoners tended to be debtors, wayward students and petty criminals.

Cranmer's martyrdom, from *Foxe's Book of Martyrs*.

Prisoners were known as Bocardo Birds. It was customary for these inmates to lower a hat on a rope from the window to entice alms from passers-by who had to walk under the very narrow gateway beneath. Some old prints suggest this receptacle was permanently hanging at the side of the gateway. During this pathetic beggary they would cry 'pity the Bocardo Birds!' or 'pray remember the Bocardo Birds!'

During the painful divorce proceedings of King Henry VIII and his first wife Katherine of Aragon, several prominent women in Oxford showed their support for the Queen by making public protests. For their troubles and loyalty thirty of them were imprisoned in the Bocardo.

The old prison was sold by the city in 1771 to the official body responsible for national highway improvements, for £306. They demolished it, causing the Bocardo Birds to fly the nest. The old door of the cell was moved to the new gaol by three-times Oxford Mayor Alderman Fisher as a memorial to the Oxford Martyrs, with an inscription and images of the three men 'ingeniously burnt in wood by a young man of the city.'

The role of St Michael's Church as a prison makes more sense when you realise that it was once part of the city defences, a watch tower on the old city walls.

The Bodleian Library

When King James I visited the Bodleian Library Schools Quad on his first Oxford visit in 1603, the sun was blazing, which seemed an auspicious sign. But James was nothing if not contrary, and, complaining that the gold gilt on the figures in the Quad dazzled him, he ordered them to be 'whitened over'. Ironically, the creators of the King James Bible (written at this man's command) compared James to the rising sun in all its glory. Detractors muttered that he was more like a bucket of whitewash. James still squints across the Schools Quad: his effigy is above the gateway, holding the famous Bible that became the voice and poetry of the Anglican Church for the next 350 years.

King James I in effigy at the Bodleian.

Folklore maintains that this Bible fell from James' effigy's stony hand in 1865 when William Gladstone, Prime Minister and Christ Church alumnus, lost his University of Oxford parliamentary seat. His drop in popularity was attributed to his support for the disestablishment of the

Church in Britain – something that horrified the average Oxford Tory. This pro-status quo movement was, and is, known as antidisestablishmentarianism. Gladstone successfully disestablished the Anglican Church of Ireland in 1871, and Wales was similarly liberated in 1914. England is still holding on, despite Anglicanism being at a low ebb.

Space was an issue at the Bodleian from the early days. An ever-growing collection (and since 1911 the Bodleian has taken a copy of every book printed in English) requires never-ending shelf space. Between the main library and the Radcliffe Camera (which the Library annexed in 1860) there is a subterranean, two-storey extension, built 1909–12 to accommodate a million books.

Work on the New Bodleian started in 1937, with a building designed by George Gilbert Scott. 60 per cent of the shelving space was underground in this innovative but unlovely building, with a tunnel connecting Old and New. The New Bodleian closed in July 2011, gutted and redesigned on the inside, and reopened as the Wilton Library. The latest extension is in faraway Swindon, in Wiltshire (the original plan to build on Osney Mead having been turned down by the council and vocal locals).

In 2010 the former Oxford University Library Services was renamed The Bodleian Libraries, bringing the magic of the Bodleian brand to the entire university.

Tom Tower, Christ Church

Tom Tower is the square tower with octagonal top that sits over Tom Gate in front of Tom Quad facing St Aldates. Designed by Christopher Wren and built 1681–82, it is one of most iconic architectural features of the city. It was not always universally admired, however. Early in the twentieth century a prominent architect was asked to submit plans to repair the time-worn tower. Instead he

Tom Tower, Christ Church.

submitted plans along Victorian Gothic lines to replace the tower entirely, arguing that no one would mourn 'so anomalous a structure' as Wren's famous folly.

The 'Tom' tag comes from the tower's bell, Great Tom. The original was hung at Osney Abbey (not St Frideswide's Priory, the Christ Church site's older incarnation, note) and was dedicated to St Thomas of Canterbury (Thomas Beckett), hence the later 'Tom' tag – it was originally called 'Mary' which was far too Catholic for the new Church of England. The bell was rescued from the Abbey after the Dissolution of the Monasteries and installed at Christ Church. Under Catholic Queen Mary I there were plans to rename it *Pulcra Maria*, 'Blessed Mary', to honour both the Queen and the Virgin Mary, but the Tom tag remained.

The bell has been recast several times, most recently in 1680 when it was inscribed with 'Great Thomas the door closer of Oxford' (in Latin). It was rehung in 1953.

A local traditional Morris tune named 'Old Tom of Oxford' is in honour of the bell. It has been recorded many times over the years, notably by Martin Carthy on *Crown of Horn* (1976) and most recently on *The Mother of All Morris* by Ashley Hutchings (2009).

During the First World War all the bells and clocks of Oxford were forbidden to chime as it was thought the chiming towers would act as a beacon for raiding Zeppelins. Even Great Tom was silent. The ploy was successful, and the city escaped any war damage. On 11 November 1918, the sound of Great Tom ringing was said to symbolise the Armistice for Oxford residents in a way no mere announcement of ceasefire could have done.

The Sheldonian Theatre

The Sheldonian will be 350 years old in 2019. It is the symbolic heart of the university. Degrees are handed out here and Chancellors are inaugurated on the premises. Inside there are grandiose portraits of King George IV, flanked by the Tsar of Russia and the Emperor of Prussia. This is a snapshot of the triumphal mood of the early nineteenth century, when the armies of these three leaders had combined to defeat Napoleon Bonaparte. The architect of George's part in that victory, Arthur Wellesley, the 'Iron' Duke of Wellington, was one of the aforesaid Chancellors, taking up the reins here in 1834. It was said that if the Sheldonian had come to grief on that day, the English Tory elite, all gathered therein, would have been extinguished. As it was, the only hiccoughs came when the Duke put his academical cap on the wrong way round, and messed up his Latin speech.

The building was financed by Gilbert Sheldon (1598–1677) and designed by Christopher Wren (his second major work). It was allegedly based on an engraving of the first century BC Theatre of Marcellus in Rome. Joseph Wells wrote in 1920, 'Architecturally it marks the first complete flowering of the genius of Sir Christopher

Sheldonian Theatre, north front, in around 1700.

Wren.' Wren was thirty-seven, Oxford's Professor of Astronomy, and renowned for his scientific skills above his architectural ones, according to Wells. He might be underplaying Wren's fame, however, as the Sheldonian project was given to him at the same time as another little task – the rebuilding of London landmarks following the Great Fire in 1666.

Radcliffe Camera

John Radcliffe did not live to see the iconic Radcliffe Camera in Oxford. It was built with money bequeathed by him on his death in 1714, to house a medical library (Radcliffe being the physician who opened the first city infirmary, and after whom the modern John Radcliffe hospital is named). The Camera was built by James Gibbs between 1737 and 1749, after he beat Nicholas Hawksmoor for the job. It is perhaps the most iconic – and photographed – structure in the city today, at the heart of the cobbled Radcliffe Square, with colleges and University Cathedral glowing all around in Cotswold stone.

One of the best times to see this dazzling magnificence is early on May Day Morning, when revellers and Morris Men crowd the cobbles to welcome the Oxford summer.

Radcliffe Infirmary

Opened in 1770, the Radcliffe Infirmary was the world's first hospital founded as a charity to treat people who would otherwise not be able to afford it. The original institution excluded children, pregnant women and people with infectious diseases, although later benefactors plugged most of these gaps. The Infirmary closed in 2007, and began a new life in 2012 as university academic offices

Radcliffe Infirmary.

at the heart of the Radcliffe Observatory Quarter – the biggest building and redevelopment project in Oxford since the nineteenth century.

The Radcliffe Observatory

The Radcliffe Observatory opened its eyes to the heavens in 1773, its aim being to further our understanding of the universe. It was, at the time, one of the foremost scientific buildings in Europe. The original idea came from Thomas Hornsby, university Professor of Astronomy in 1763. He had observed the 1769 transit of Venus – an astronomical event of great fame – from a room at the Bodleian Tower, and the event had such a great impact on him that he appealed to the trustees of John Radcliffe (who had already funded the Radcliffe Camera and Radcliffe Infirmary) to pay for an observatory.

The original architect, Henry Keene, had designed a rather dull, square tower. Fortunately, he was succeeded by James Wyatt who came up with the irregular octagonal version, based on an engraving of the Tower of the Winds in Athens. There are representations of the eight winds by sculptor John Bacon around the top of the structure.

After slow decline, the last astronomers abandoned the building in 1934. It was taken over by the Nuffield Institute of Medical Research after William Morris (Lord Nuffield) purchased the observatory and donated it back to the university. It found new purpose as the nucleus of the Oxford Medical School, a role it maintained until 1970 (in spite of its architectural unsuitability for such a role).

Restoration work between 2004 and 2012 gave the building a phoenix-like facelift, and it is now the pride and joy of Green Templeton College. The grounds, meanwhile, have hardly changed since the original landscaping.

Oxford's Covered Market

In 1776 a local guidebook claimed that the Covered Market was 'universally allowed to exceed everything of its kind in the kingdom.' John Betjemen concurred in the 1950s, claiming that its Georgian air somehow made anything bought there seem better quality than stuff from other shops.

Novelist and Magdalen College alumnus Jonathan Keates (born 1946) saw more of a mixed bag in 'the wondrous Covered Market', describing it as 'a Levantine bazaar' with 'hucksters peddling everything from birdseed to baguettes.'

The site was chosen after the 1771 Mileways Act outlawed street trading in St Aldates, which had been the main market area of Oxford (as Fish Street). Drugs and spices were sold from street stalls on the site of the new market, and some old university halls occupied the plot too. The edifice today is largely the work of Thomas Wyatt the Younger in 1890. But even this second version has not remained entirely safe from redevelopment. A lobby in the

1940s pressed for a Covered Market Mark III, complaining of the 'gloomy and congested' atmosphere, and claiming that 'the carrying of bloody carcasses across crowded pavements does not increase their pleasantness'.

The Ashmolean Museum

The old Ashmolean Museum opened on 24 May 1683, in the building that now functions as The Museum of the History of Science on Broad Street. The original Ashmolean collection predates this site by fifty years, however. It began as a collection of artworks, curios and nick-nacks in the Upper Reading room of the Bodleian Library, added to by various donors including Archbishop Laud in the 1630s. The non-art side of the collection was largely based on a 'Cabinet of Curiosities' put together by John Tradescant in Lambeth, London, earlier in the century. Known as Tradescant's Ark, the ragbag included a dodo, carved cherry stones, and Biblical Joseph's coat of many colours.

The museum's founder, Elias Ashmole, donated his money on the condition that his collection – he had been bequeathed Tradescant's Ark – should have its own custom-built museum. The first curator, or keeper, was Dr Robert Plot, who presided over an institution that included exhibits, a chemistry laboratory and lecture rooms for undergraduates. The art collection remained at the Bodleian, but it soon required an extension to house its growing canvases, bronzes and statuary.

In 1845 the new museum on Beaumont Street opened to accommodate the burgeoning art collection, along with the Greek and Roman statues that still dominate the ground floor of the museum (gifted by the Countess of Pomfret in 1755). The original art was ousted over the years in favour of noteworthy artists and an important collection of Old Master drawings, including the work of da Vinci, Michelangelo and Raphael (paid for by public subscription). In 1861 a group of J.W.M. Turner paintings was acquired. Uccello's *The Hunt in the Forest*, one of the major pieces in the modern museum, was donated along with other early Italian works in 1851 by the splendidly named William Thomas Horner Fox-Strangeways.

The poor old Ashmolean on Broad Street was now in disrepair. The stuffed specimens had been destroyed by collection-devouring Dermestid beetles, the cabinets were falling apart, and much of the original Ark had lost its appeal in an increasingly scientific age. It was overhauled as a proto-natural history museum (known as natural theology in those days) displaying the fruits of creation.

When this large element of the collection found its own dedicated home at the Museum of Natural History, the remaining artefacts became the focus of an archaeological and historical museum. The appointment of Arthur Evans as keeper in 1884, pre-eminent archaeologist of his age, consolidated this incarnation of the Ashmolean; but

Broad Street.

his eager acquisition of around 2,000 new artefacts a year, along with ongoing donations, finally pushed the collection out of the Broad Street building. In 1894 it was reunited with the old art collection, and in 1908 the two wings merged to become the institution as we know it today – The Ashmolean Museum of Art and Archaeology.

The last great leap took place in 2010, with an extension that doubled the display area of the museum and created new education and conservation spaces, not to mention a much-feted rooftop café.

The University Museum of Natural History

The museum is a Grade I listed neo-Gothic building, completed in 1861. The stone columns inside the edifice are each constructed from different English rocks, chosen by the first keeper of the museum, John Phillips. The stone flora and fauna that decorate the building inside and out were the work of James and John O'Shea, along with their nephew Edward Whelan, renowned carvers from Ireland (the building having been designed by Irish architects). Although the museum was funded by the university, the decoration was funded by public subscription. Inevitably, money ran out and much of the work was never completed.

When the funds dried up, the O'Sheas generously offered to continue working unpaid, only to be accused of defacing the building with 'freehand' additions. Their wonderful response was to caricature their critics in the university by carving them as parrots and owls – these can be seen in the prominent panel over the building's entrance. Pre-eminent Oxford scientist Henry Acland, the man who had originally planned the construction of the new museum, asked them to remove the recognisable human heads from the carved birds.

Historian William Tuckwell recalled the O'Sheas: 'Every morning came the handsome red-bearded Irish brothers Shea, bearing plants from the Botanic Garden, to reappear under their chisels in the rough-hewn capitals of the pillars.'

The adjoining Pitt Rivers Museum was completed in 1886. At the time it was thought important to keep the work of man (i.e. General Augustus Pitt-Rivers' anthropological collection) from the work of God, which is why a separate entity was needed rather than a simple extension.

Maxwell House

Headington Hill Hall, in the leafy setting of Headington Hill Park, is owned by the city council. Since 1992 it has been leased by Oxford Brookes University, and has been described as the most expensive council house in the country. It is occupied by Brookes' School of Law and the joint Brookes/Oxford University Oxford Institute of Legal Practice.

The house was built in 1824 for local brewing magnates the Morrell family, with an Italianate 1858 extension. The Morrells kept residence for 114 years and were renowned for their huge parties. In 1959 the house was rented to Robert Maxwell (1923–1991), acquiring the nickname Maxwell House. Born in Czechoslovakia as Jan Ludvík Hyman Binyamin Hoch, Maxwell owned the *Daily Mirror* newspaper and founded Pergamon Press; but he is far more famous for his dubious financial practices and his death, falling from a yacht in a classic 'did he jump or was he pushed?' drama.

The Bridge of Sighs

The Bridge of Sighs surprises many visitors who assume it has been there for centuries. It was designed (largely) by Sir Thomas Jackson, and completed in 1914 to link two sections of Hertford College. Its official name is Hertford Bridge and, despite popular folklore, was not supposed to be a copy of the Bridge of Sighs in Venice (or indeed the Rialto Bridge, which it more closely resembles).

The bridge nearly failed at the planning stage when the Town (the city council) was unhappy with the idea of the Gown (the university) bridging a public thoroughfare. A long lawsuit followed, and the Gown successfully asserted its rights by producing relevant charters, some going back to King John in the thirteenth century.

It wasn't only the Town who objected. The Warden of New College opposed the plans, saying it would obscure the view of his college's bell tower from that end of New College Lane.

Said Business School

The glass-fronted Said Business School, near the railway station, is part of Green Templeton College. It is the venue of one of Oxford's best-kept secrets: a rooftop amphitheatre where actors do battle with ambient noise from road, rail and air traffic on summer evenings (unless rain banishes disgruntled spectators and players to the indoor lecture theatre below). The school has the city's newest 'dreaming spire', a truncated green structure completed in 1996.

Oxford Brookes University

Between 2010 and 2014, drastic rebuilding took place at the central site of Oxford Brookes University, off London Road and Gipsy Lane. This was all taken at a bit of a dash following the usual wrestling matches with local council and residents. At one point demolition

Bridge of Sighs, a surprisingly recent addition to Oxford's architecture.

was taking place before the final go-ahead for the new building had been given.

A Blue Plaque commemorating the institution's founder John Henry Brookes (1891–1975) was unveiled in 2011 at his former home at No. 195 The Slade, Headington. Brookes was Vice Principal of the newly formed and badly named 'Oxford City Technical School, incorporating the School of Art', in 1934. This was a merger between a couple of nineteenth-century institutions. It became Oxford Polytechnic in 1970, and Oxford Brookes University (usually shortened to Brookes) in 1992. In addition to the central site in Headington, it also has wings in Harcourt Hill and Wheatley, 6 miles apart.

Chapter Five

Statues and Memorials

From kings, queens and college founders to dogs, sharks and naked men, Oxford is populated by statuesque over-seers and pockmarked with memorial stones. These are the highlights…

Murdered Monarchs

Two doomed kings adorn the Quad at Oriel College: Edward II and Charles I. The former was dethroned and murdered in 1327. Though legend insists that he was skewered on a red hot poker, more sober historians reckon he was suffocated. There are further effigies and portraits of Edward at the college.

Stuart king Charles I was famously beheaded, after using Oxford as his HQ during the English Civil Wars in the seventeenth century.

Lots More Stuarts

Pembroke College Hall has a statue of King James I, and the college arms bear a red rose and a thistle, symbolis-ing the union of England and Scotland under James. Charles I and Charles II can be seen lording it over the Botanic Gardens, in the twin statues guarding the gateway designed by Inigo Jones. Further down the High on the front of University College, Stuart matriarch's Mary (1662–1694) and Anne (1665–1714) can be seen. The latter is accompanied by Dr John Radcliffe, of Radcliffe Camera and Hospital fame (see p.116). Queen Anne also turns up in Tom Quad at Christ Church, keeping company with Cardinal Wolsey and

King Charles I.

Bishop Fell, the man responsible for the college's Tom Tower and Quad.

James II is the rarest monarch to be found in stone; the unpopular Catholic king was deposed, and all traces of him tended to be removed. This surviving statue, on the interior-side of the High Street-facing western gateway (the one with Anne on the street side) at University College, is therefore a great rarity.

More Queens

Over the road from Anne and Mary, the eighteenth-century cupola (a kind of stone cage) rising above Queen's College contains an effigy of Caroline of Brunswick, wife of King George II. The college was named after one of Royalty's earlier consorts, Queen Philippa of Hainault (1314–1369), wife of Edward III. The wives of kings have been patrons here ever since. The college motto is *Reginae erunt nutrices tuae*, meaning 'Queens shall be thy nursing mothers' (a quote from the book of Isaiah in the Bible).

Hail Mary

The most controversial of Oxford's Queens was the Queen of Heaven herself, the Virgin Mary. In the eighteenth century her statue was restored to its traditional niche over the entrance to New College on New College lane. The aperture is very low, forcing visitors to bow their heads before entering. This is said to have been a Catholic jest, or a form of revenge, ensuring that all visitors bowed before the Virgin. Puritans were apoplectic, of course, but the statue survived. The city's most prominent alternative Virgin Mary stands over the south porch of the eponymous St Mary's Church on the High Street.

Merton College

Merton has a fifteenth-century 3D frieze above its entrance. The scene depicts John the Baptist (college patron), Walter de Merton (college founder), and a stony landscape with trees and animals, including a unicorn (see p.73).

Apart from the famous Bodleian library, the chief memorial to Thomas Bodley is the statue in Merton chapel. Created by the aptly named Nicholas Stone, it depicts Bodley with piles of books, and some female attendants representing the teaching faculties.

Magdalen College

The statue collection over Magdalen College chapel's west door features: John the Baptist (the college being built on the site of the St John Hospital), Mary Magdalen (for obvious reasons), William of Waynflete (Bishop of Winchester and college founder), St Swithun (who, like Waynflete, was Bishop of Winchester, and got his own Quad at the college in the late nineteenth century) and King Edward IV (king at the time of the foundation).

Saints go marching in

Fans of the Saints (the holy men, not the football team) are spoilt for choice in Oxford. All Souls, Magdalen and New College all have restored reredos screens on their altar walls, enormous stone lattices with honeycombs of niches, each containing the statue of a saint. Needless to say, these works of art did not escape the attentions of the Puritans in the seventeenth century, but the screens were restored in the mid-nineteenth century.

Le Sueur's Bronze Age

The bronze statue of the Earl of Pembroke (University Chancellor, 1617–30) in the School's Quadrangle of the Bodleian was made by Hubert Le Sueur (1580–1658). It was a conscious effort to revive the bronze-working skills of the Greeks and Romans. Le Sueur is also responsible for the bronze effigies of Charles I and consort Queen Henrietta, made for Chancellor William Laud in 1634. They can be seen facing each other across the beautiful Canterbury Quad at St John's.

Natural Historians

The main court of the Oxford University Museum of Natural History has some heavyweight overseers. Encircling you along the four walls are statues and busts of scientists, engineers and philosophers, most of them having worked and studied in Oxford at some point.

The museum was designed on the sort of scale normally reserved for religious edifices – its lofty ironwork arches and magnificent stonework echo the scale and contours of a Gothic cathedral. It represents a time when religion and science were still able to shout coherently across a crowded room, its natural history content originally intended to proclaim the work of a supernatural creator.

Times have moved on, in scientific circles at least, but the legends of science are still here in stony repose. The likes of Darwin, Newton and Linnaeus are sculpted from French Caen limestone with a symbol of their life's work (for example, Newton has an apple, representing the one which fell on his head with such gravity, and William Harvey, who first worked out the mechanics of blood circulation, holds a human heart).

The sculpting was planned on a grand scale, and was to be paid for by private subscription. There is room for thirty-five figures in all, ranging from Hippocrates (died *c.* 377 BC) down to Walter Frank Raphael Weldon, Linacre Professor of Comparative Anatomy (died 1906). But the work was never completed. Only nineteen statues were produced (including a cheeky Prince Albert to please Queen Victoria), with a further nine busts commissioned on the cheap to shore up some of the gaps.

The Emperors

Oxford's most famous statues are probably the mysterious 'Emperors', thirteen alarming-looking giant busts surrounding the Sheldonian Theatre. Battered by wind and rain, the current crop is the third set to sit here, carved in the early 1970s by Michael Black. They replaced the Emperors of 1868, which were of poor quality stone, and, to add to the problem, were routinely defaced by students. In 1925 poet John Betjemen described them as 'mouldering busts'.

Next to the Sheldonian on the Clarendon Building, the Nine Muses cast an inspiring eye over the city.

Ogle at the Taylor Institute

The four large statues that decorate the tops of the Doric columns outside the Taylor Institute on St Giles were said (scurrilously, it would appear) to be based on four young women, surnamed Ogle, who lived nearby. The statues represent the literary heritage of Germany, France, Italy and Spain. The building was opened in 1845, funded with money left by architect Sir Robert Taylor (1714–1788), and functions as the university's foreign languages library.

Watch Dog

Another eye-catching character can be seen above the doorway of Payne & Son Silversmiths at No. 131 High Street. It is an imposing white-painted bronze Great Dane, holding a giant fob watch in his teeth. The watch used to have painted hands but, according to the current manager, these were painted out because people kept calling into the shop to say 'your clock has stopped, it's not telling the correct time!' Sadly, no one seems to recall the inspiration behind the dog (if, indeed, it is more than a simple visual pun on 'watch dog'). It was already there when Paynes moved into the premises in 1889, and was formerly painted brown (or possibly plain

Great Dane statue on High Street.

bronze) before whitewashing in the mid-twentieth century. It was probably commissioned by James Sheard, a watch-maker and jeweller who owned the premises in the 1860s.

Martyr's Memorial

George Gilbert Scott's Martyrs Memorial on St Giles in Oxford was not erected as a spontaneous gesture of sorrow and affection towards the unfortunate threesome burned at the stake by Mary I (see p.27). Archbishops Cranmer, Latimer and Ridley – the Martyrs in question – had died for the principles of the Protestant Reformation, and in 1830s Oxford these principles were judged to be under threat. Not only was Catholic emancipation now a reality, but all manner of Low Church alternatives to the Church of England were muddying the holy waters too.

Subscribers to the memorial project (for this is how it was funded) were left in no doubt of what it represented, due to the carefully worded inscription that was circulated as part of the pre-building money raising effort, and which can be read on site today. It mentions the Anglican martyrs and 'the sacred truths which they had affirmed and maintained against the errors of the Church of Rome'.

Some of the project's critics were scathing. A.W.N. Pugin, a giant of a figure in architecture and father of the Victorian Gothic revival, issued a pamphlet denouncing it. He spoke of the 'atrocities' committed by the so-called martyrs under their own anti-Catholic tenure, and described the proposed memorial as a puny construction in a city 'which owes its very existence to Catholic piety'.

The controversial project ran into financial trouble, but Gilbert was magnanimous enough to forgo part of his fee. Since then the memorial, completed in 1843, has become a famous landmark, its anti-Catholic sentiments largely forgotten. It is also the object of a traditional practical joke, in which visitors and newcomers to the city are told that the spire-like memorial is actually the top of a subterranean church.

Gill and Epstein

Sculpture has some great twentieth-century secrets in Oxford, including Eric Gill's St John in the Wilderness on the inside of the gate house at St John's, and his Stations of the Cross at St Alban's Church in East Oxford. The carved lettering on the war memorial in New College's chapel is also by Gill, as is the lettering on the monolith outside South Park.

New College also boasts Jacob Epstein's Lazarus, a rather alarming mummy-like figure in bandages, depicting the man raised from the dead by Jesus in the New Testament. As an illustration of its power, after a visit to Oxford in the 1960s, Russian Communist Chairman Nikita Khrushchev said that the memory of this sculpture would keep him awake at night.

In front of the former church of St Peter-in-the-East on Queen's Lane is a statue of Saint Edmund of Abingdon, looking abstract, thin and studious. It was created by Rodney Munday in 2007 to mark the 50th anniversary of the modern St Edmund's Hall.

Why?

In the twenty-first century, sculpture has continued to make its mark. Y, a two-dimensional steel tree erection by Mark Wallinger, stands amidst the trees at Bat Willow Meadow, Magdalen College. It was commissioned to mark the institution's 550th anniversary in 2008 and was positioned to reflect the setting of the midsummer sun. As to the question 'Why Y?', it combines the mathematical reference of the vertical 'y'-axis, (one of the three axes of a three-dimensional Cartesian coordinate system) and the male Y-chromosome of DNA. It also echoes the Greek letter upsilon (which resembles a Y), a symbol that also represents the number 400. In medieval Roman numerals, Y was given a value of 150, and so the sum total is 550. Possibly the most obscure reference to an anniversary of all time!

Another time, another nude

The century's other celebrated erection is Anthony Gormley's nude man on the roof of Blackwell's Art and Poster shop, on the corner of Broad and Turl Streets. The 7ft half-tonne iron work landed here in 2009.

It is part of a series by Gormley (creator of the Angel of the North) and is called Another Time II. It was purchased by Exeter College after an anonymous donor offered the money (in excess of £250,000).

Anthony Gormley statue on Turl Street. (Photograph by Jan Sullivan)

All did not go smoothly for the nude man. Unsurprisingly, some objected to the full frontal effrontery, and ten days before the unveiling ceremony, po-faced councillors announced that the statue did not have planning permission. The local newspapers enjoyed the dilemma, but the Mayoress allowed the unveiling to go ahead, noting: 'It's not unusual to apply for retrospective planning permission.'

Memorial stones and monuments

The Peace Stone set in the north side of Carfax Tower reads: 'Peace was proclaimed in Oxford'. It is a little puzzling on first glance, as the inscribed date has been almost weathered away. It used to read June 27 1814, which only adds to the confusion – what peace, you may well ask, was worth a memorial stone in 1814? It is a little bubble in time. 1814 was the year in which Napoleon Bonaparte was imprisoned on Elba, the Treaty of Paris was signed, and the Napoleonic wars seemed to be over. The French Emperor escaped, however, and it was not until the following year, at Waterloo, that the real peace arrived.

There is another Peace Stone in the unlikely setting of the Plain roundabout, where four roads meet just beyond Magdalen Bridge. The stone has a lamppost on top, and looks like a small tomb. This is explained by its original position, in the cemetery of St Clement's Church. The stone has not actually moved: a surviving section of the churchyard was isolated when the church was demolished in 1829 (with a replacement built around the same time at the south end of Marston Road), and levelled in 1950 when the roundabout was constructed. This relic now sits, unread and unloved, as one of the stone blocks that circle the roundabout. Another commemorates the lost churchyard.

Oxford's first Methodist meeting house, founded by John Wesley himself, is marked in stone on the surviving building in New Inn Hall Street, depicting Wesley and his famous flowing locks.

A memorial plaque to soldiers Piggs and Biggen can be seen at Gloucester Green. The men were shot here in 1649 for their part in the Second Mutiny of the Oxford Garrison, part of

Cromwell.

the Levellers movement (main tenets – a socially extended democracy, equality in law and religious tolerance). They are symbols both of the Levellers and of Oliver Cromwell's take-no-prisoners approach to all things military.

The foundation stone of the Town Hall stands on the corner of Blue Boar Street off St Aldates. It notes that the stone was laid by Mayor Thomas Lucas and Sheriff Thomas Taphouse on 6 July 1893, the wedding day of the Duke of York and Princess Victoria Mary of Teck. What it doesn't mention is that the half-ton block had to be laid twice. The original stone included the name of the builder John S. Chappel of Pimlico, who went bankrupt three months after the foundation stone was in place. Not wishing to immortalise such an ill-starred name, the stone was dragged out and re-inscribed with the replacement builders John Parnell & Sons, then relaid with minimal fuss.

A squat monolith on the London Road side of South Park (inscribed by Eric Gill) commemorates the purchase of these fifty-four acres of ancient, open green space by the Oxfordshire Preservation Trust in December 1932. The plot was sold for £23,155 (about £800,000 in today's money) on condition that no building should ever be erected on it. In 1951 the Preservation Trust gave the park to the City of Oxford for public use.

The New Bodleian Library on Parks Road and Broad Street has a plaque explaining, in good twentieth-century Oxford Latin, that Queen Mary, mother of King George VI, laid the foundation stone on 25 June 1937. Unloved on account of its rather utilitarian appearance, the building suffered a bad omen when, in 1940, George VI came to formally open the library. He inserted the key into the lock, and it snapped in two. The building has recently been gutted and rearranged on the inside, and will reopen as the Weston Library in 2015, hopefully attended by more auspicious omens.

'Studies serve for delight, for ornament and for abilities' reads the stone inscription over the door of the former public library at the side of the Town Hall on Blue Boar Street. The quote is from Francis Bacon's essay 'Of Studies'. The library moved into this building in 1897 and left again in 1973. The premises were used by the Museum of Oxford until 2011. The museum is currently installed in the Town Hall.

'Clarendon House' is proclaimed in stone on the east side of Cornmarket. Beneath the name is a puzzling letter W that looks like two decorative saws, with the date 1957. This stands for 'Woolworth' – the Oxford branch first opened in 1924, and moved to this building in 1957.

At No.3 Merton Street is a stone plaque reading, 'In this house was born Col. Henry Marten Gentleman Commoner of University College, Oxford, MP for Berkshire, Republican and Wit. 1602–1680.' Lawyer and politician, he is most famous for regicide as one of the men who signed the death warrant of King Charles I.

Possibly the most obscure message is to be found in the inscription on Oriel College's imposing Rhodes Building on the High Street, beneath the statue of Cecil Rhodes. It reads: *E: L A R G A : M V Nn I F I C E N T I A C A E C I L I I : R H O D E S*. In English this means 'as a result of the munificence of Cecil Rhodes'. But there is a hidden message. Some of the capital letters of the inscription are larger than others (in italics in the quoted Latin above), giving the sequence LMVIICICILIID. These are supposed to be rearranged to MDCCCLLVIIIIII to solve the puzzle. This sequence translates from Roman numerals as 1911, the date of the building's foundation, and the beginning of the flourishing history of Rhodes Scholars at the university. However, the year would normally be written MCMXI, which makes the conundrum even sillier.

Shark bombshell

A spectacular seven metre fibreglass great white shark juts out alarmingly from the roof of a Victorian house in New High Street, Headington. It was installed by Radio Oxford DJ and former Balliol law student Bill Heine in 1986, redefining the old 'you either love it or hate it' argument.

The shark's original designation was 'Untitled 1986', unveiled on the 41st anniversary of the dropping of the atomic bomb on Nagasaki, and intended as a statement of anger and impotence in the face of the madness of the modern world. It was created by sculptor John Buckley, and has survived Oxford City Council attempts to get the structure condemned. It remains one of the most remarkable sights in Oxford and the unofficial emblem of Headington.

A second shark appeared in Headington in 2011, decorating the top of the fish and chip shop on London Road.

Headington shark.

It had a relatively easy ride through planning permission, probably because of the precedence of Bill Heine's creature and the fact that Headington has embraced the shark as its unlikely mascot.

Chapter Six

Inns
and Outs

Remnants of several long-gone university inns, halls and colleges can be seen scattered throughout the city. An ancient arched gateway and wall on New Inn Hall Street are the surviving bits of Frewin Hall, founded in 1421 as St Mary's College. The current, rebuilt Frewin Hall belongs to Brasenose College. It was here that the mighty academic Erasmus stayed in the 1490s, and where the somewhat less academically gifted Prince Albert Edward (King Edward VII) lodged nearly 400 years later.

New Inn Hall, another of the university's many long-gone pre-college halls, was, along with Rose Hall, the basis for St Peter's College (on the opposite side of the road from the Frewin remnants). Both of these halls were founded in the thirteenth century, and bits of them still survive in the college grounds.

Kemp Hall, founded in 1637, is one of the later 'lost' university foundations. It survives as a Thai restaurant, stretching along a passage at No. 130a High Street, with a frontage on the main road. Tackley Inn, further along the High Street, is another fine example.

Thirteen centuries at Port Meadow

Port Meadow, to the north-east of Oxford, has not changed since the city was first founded. It is said to have been given to the Freemen of Oxford for their part in fighting off the Danish army in the late ninth century. Port Meadow consists of 120 hectares (300 acres) of unenclosed common, is prone to flooding and is a haven of wildlife, day-trippers and grazing cattle and horses. Some areas of Oxford still enjoy grazing rights on the Meadow, and on Wolvercote Common to the north.

In the seventeenth and eighteenth centuries, the tranquility was occasionally broken by organised horse racing, and during the First World War it was a military airfield and Royal Artillery base. In 1940 the war connection was continued, with a camp set up to receive battered personnel evacuated from Dunkirk.

Ditching the old name

The city ditch used to run along what is now Broad Street, between the city wall and Balliol and Trinity Colleges. You would imagine it was filled with all manner of nasty things, but seventeenth-century historian Anthony Wood says it once had a stream named *Candida fossa*, 'clear stream'. The lane which led to the ditch (the western section of Broad Street between Waterstones book shop and the far edge of Balliol College) was called Canditch, after the stream. In the earliest records, this part of the street is called Horsemonger Lane, and was the site of an annual horse-trader's fair.

The stream was presumably long gone in Wood's time, as the ditch had been dry enough in the previous century to allow the burning of the Oxford martyrs on large bonfires (see p.27).

Jewish memorials

The old Jewish quarter of Oxford was obliterated long ago. Jews first arrived here in 1080, based in an area on and around St Aldates and Blue Boar Street. The street was known as Great Jewry Street on the strength of their presence, at the commercial heart of the city. Banned from following standard trades, mediaeval Oxford's Jews made their living from medicine, pawn-brokerage, money lending and property. Early students at the university relied on them for accommodation and loans. The Jews themselves were not allowed to study at the university.

These trades do not endear themselves to a populace. This was the Jews' catch-22 situation, forced by legislation into trades that, although essential services, built resentment. Things came to a head in the thirteenth century, when attacks on Jews throughout England became more frequent. The Oxford Ascension Day riot of 1268 started after a Jewish man was accused of mocking a university religious procession and trampling on a crucifix. The entire community was rounded up and arrested, and punished by being forced to fund a marble and gold crucifix for Merton College.

On 18 July 1290, King Edward I expelled all Jews from England. Many had left already, and in 1290 only ten Jewish property holders were left in Oxford. Their property was confiscated, and the Great Jewry became Fish Street. Tradition maintains that some Jews converted to Christianity in order to stay in Oxford, and produced Bibles in Hebrew and Latin.

Jews were allowed back to the city in the seventeenth century. Some were employed cataloguing Hebrew manuscripts at the Bodleian Library, or taught Hebrew to students. One, called Jacob (or Cirques Jobson), made his mark by opening Oxford's first coffee house in 1650.

A community had built up in St Clements by the 1730s, beyond the city boundary and away from the anti-Semitic jurisdiction of the university. There was a community of Catholics in the area too.

Only in 1856 were Jews allowed to study at the university. Around 9 per cent of college members today are Jewish, and there is an Oxford Centre for Jewish Studies, based at No. 45 St Giles. The medieval Jewish cemetery is commemorated with a plaque at its former site, now the university Botanic Gardens (beginning 'beneath this garden lies a medieval cemetery'). The footpath from the gardens to Christ Church Meadows, which linked the cemetery to the Jewish quarter, is still known as Dead Man's Walk. There is also a plaque commemorating the Great Jewry on Blue Boar Street, and on the wall of the Town Hall on St Aldates.

Oxford on the defensive

The Royalists had proposed elaborate defences for Oxford in 1645. According to plans drawn up by the leading Dutch engineer of the age, Sir Bernard de Gomme, the entire city and suburbs were to be enclosed by bank, ditch and walls, shaped like a gigantic star. Each straight section of the starry walls would have been as long as Cornmarket, but the plan never got beyond the first few earthworks. De Gomme also planned to dam the rivers and flood the outskirts of Oxford, transforming it into an island.

Work on his schemes was slow. Charles enlisted townsfolk but refused to pay them. As a result, of 122 pressganged navvies, only twelve turned up. University students, more pro-Royalist than the average townsman, did some of the work – it was noted by an observer that 'night and day [they] gall their hands with mattocks and shovels'.

The only remains of Civil War Royalist defence works are some earth banks between Merton and Balliol sports fields, and in gardens at Wadham College and Rhodes House. Parliamentarian lumps and bumps can be found in Old Marston, and in South Park.

Carfax – turning water into wine

The Carfax Conduit used to stand at the Carfax cross-roads, on the site of the city bull ring. Twelve metres tall and decorated with statuettes and frescoes, the structure supplied Oxford with water via lead pipes from a spring at nearby Harcourt Hill. It was built in 1617, the structure and water conduit system having been designed by Otho Nicholson, a lawyer and Christ Church man, when the thirteenth-century water pipes fell into disrepair.

The conduit performed its services for more than a century and a half. The following was written after its repair in 1686:

> The water which comes from the fountain head or conduit-house near Hinksey aforementioned is conveyed into the body of the carved ox, and thereby the city is supplied with good and whole-some water, issuing from his pizzle, which continually pisses into the cistern underneath from whence proceeds a leaden pipe out of which runs wine on extraordinary days of rejoycing.

The restoration of the monarchy in 1660 was one occasion when water was turned into wine.

The conduit was removed in 1787, as it was blocking traffic, and was replaced with a more discrete water cistern. The Harcourt family of Stanton Harcourt rescued the folly for their Nuneham Courtney estate. Their park was redesigned by 'Capability' Brown in the 1790s, whose plans had included a neo-Gothic tower overlooking the

Thames, but the Harcourts decided to use the defunct Carfax Conduit instead. It can still be seen in their grounds.

Oxford's conduit system began to dry up in the nineteenth century (limescale from the hard water being a perennial problem) and in 1869 the small replacement conduit at Carfax was sold by the university to the Oxford Corporation, who removed it. A defunct drinking fountain in the wall of St Martin's tower is all that remains. The building called Conduit House, at Harcourt Hill, marks the original spring, and is looked after by English Heritage.

Run of the mill

Demolished in 2004, the papermill on the Thames at Lower Wolvercote in the Oxford suburbs used to supply the Oxford University Press and provide the material upon which *Jackson's Oxford Journal* (1782–1928) was printed. Powered solely by the Thames until 1811, it then utilised a steam engine requiring a staggering 100 tons of coal a week. The main purpose of the Oxford Canal was to transport coal for such purposes as this.

The old mill stream is crossed by a former toll bridge now known as the Airmen's Bridge, at Wolvercote. It has a plaque commemorating an accident which took place in 1912, when the adjoining Port Meadow was being used as a military airfield. Two officers of the Royal Flying Corps were killed when their plane crashed, and 2,226 Oxfordians gave money to have the plaque installed.

Clock runs slow

The Victoria Fountain on The Plain, just before the roundabout beyond Magdalen Bridge, has not flowed for many years. The feature, and its accompanying ornate Diamond Jubilee Clock, were planned to mark the

Queen's celebrations in 1897, but they were running late. The feature was not unveiled until 1899. A stone inscription explains (in Latin): 'G. Herbert Morrell M.P., together with his wife, arranged for this bridge to be provided with a clock in honour of Victoria, by the Grace of God Queen of the Britains, who now in 1897 has completed twelve lustra' (i.e. 12 x 5 years). This timely inscription is confusingly under the fountain. The fountain itself (doubling as a horse trough) has an inscription (again, translated from Latin, and, again confusingly, situated under the clock face):

'The water falls, the hour goes by, be wise and drink, seize the swift-flying time.'

Oxford's coat of arms

The coat of arms can be seen in various places throughout the city, notably in the Town Hall. The full arms (rather than the truncated 'ox crossing water' version) features the following:

The Oxford ox fording the Thames. This device crops up in many places, from lampposts to the imposing but rather lost-looking beast at the railway station.

A black elephant, symbol of seventeenth-century Sir Francis Knollys, High Steward of the City, Lord Lieutenant, and MP.

A green beaver, symbol of seventeenth-century Henry Norreys of Rycote, Captain of the City Militia, MP.

Town Hall elephant.
(Photograph by Jan Sullivan)

A leopard with blue fleurs-de-lys, crown and Tudor Rose, granted to Oxford by Queen Elizabeth I after her visit in 1566.

The motto *Fortis est Veritas*, meaning 'truth is strong'.

Sharp-eyed observers will spot the heads of elephants and beavers on the exterior lead pipes of the Town Hall. There is a colourful version of the full coat of arms in the gates at Headington Hill Hall too.

Pleasure Gardens of Rome

Rome was an area north of Oxford University Parks, roughly in the region enclosed by modern Banbury Road, Norham Gardens and Bradmore Road. It was accessed by a road called Non Ultra and centred on a low hill with a cave beneath, marked first with a stone cross, and later with a windmill and single house. Further north stood Greenditch, which contained a gallows. Rome enjoyed a brief heyday as Pleasure Gardens, but by the late nineteenth century had succumbed to housing, the main site being covered by Wycliffe Hall in 1877.

Seacourt old and new

The village of Seacourt near modern Botley was first recorded in the tenth century, when it was handed to Abingdon Abbey by King Eadwig. Legend says that at its height it had twenty-four inns, to serve the needs of pilgrims visiting the nearby St Margaret's healing well at Binsey. However, by the fifteenth century its glory days were gone: the local church collapsed in 1439, its two mills were closed, and it was noted that only two of the village's cottages were habitable. By the time Oxford historian Anthony Wood visited in the mid-seventeenth century, only a few ruins and bumps in a field indicated that a settlement had ever existed.

The name survives at the Seacourt Park and Ride. There is also a Seacourt Bridge pub on Seacourt Road, next to the Seacourt Stream, and Seacourt Tower, a metal spire on the top of a former car showroom, built 1965–66. This gives the building the semi-affectionate local name 'Botley Cathedral'.

Radcliffe Meteorological Station

The first Observer at the Radcliffe Observatory, Thomas Hornsby, made his first meteorological records in 1774. Originally the weather station sat on a wooden platform beside the Atlas-borne globe that adorns the top of the observatory. However, this position contravened the rules set by modern meteorological data collectors, and in the 1960s the station was relocated to the garden. It is the UK's longest running weather station, with temperature and rainfall measurements taken almost continuously since 1767.

Norman conquests

The tower of St George at the castle is the most famous Norman landmark in the city, but there are other Norman treasures off the beaten track. The 1170 church of St Mary

St Ebbes' Norman arch.
(Photograph by Jan Sullivan)

at Iffley has one of the finest carved Norman arch doorways in the country, featuring a series of bird-like beaked heads. The nearby weir at Iffley Lock has a set of 'rollers', enabling rowing boats and punts to be dragged to the

Iffley Lock.

next level. A neighbouring twelfth-century watermill burnt down in 1908.

The late-Victorian St Ebbe's Church in central Oxford also has a fine Norman doorway with beaked heads, restored and installed as part of the rebuild.

Bridging the gaps

The Bridge of Sighs on New College Lane, linking two sections of Hertford College, is the most well-known of Oxford's street-spanning bridges, but there are others.

Pembroke College Bridge, Brewer Street. (Photograph by Jan Sullivan)

At the St Ebbe's Street end of Brewer Street, a modern footbridge vaults the old city wall to link parts of Pembroke College. On Merton Street (known as Coach and Horse Lane prior to 1838) at the vacated premises of the former Philosophy Centre library (which moved to the Radcliffe Observatory Quarter on Woodstock Road in August 2012) opposite Merton College, a neat little modern bridge nips across the courtyard, waiting for its next lease of life.

Welcome to Paradise

On Paradise Street, looking back towards the castle from the bridge, the ghost of the former Castle Mill can be seen in the Mill Stream. It races down a short weir marking the spot where the mill wheel – and accompanying building – used to be. You can walk along much of the old Mill Stream. Nearby is an old malthouse, marked by a statue of a dog, origin unknown. The malthouse is associated with the nearby Lion Brewery on St Thomas Street, which was formerly the home of Oxford brewers Morrells. The brewery's cast-iron archway can still be seen, but the building, along with its attendant pub to the left of the archway, has been converted to flats.

Castle Mill Stream, Paradise Street.

Lion Brewery, Morrells, St Thomas Street.

Pub crawl

Completely hidden from any road, The Turf Tavern at the end of St Helen's Passage off Holywell Street is one of the city's worst kept secrets and most characterful pubs. It nestles under a section of the old city wall, and boasts head-crackingly low beams and outdoor braziers in the winter.

The Chequers, down an alley beneath the stone 'watch dog' at No. 131 High Street, has a suitably chequered history, recorded in a plaque on the wall. It was a private house from 1260 to 1434, after which it was occupied by a money lender. He used the traditional Roman money-lender's sign of a chequered board. Part of the building became an inn in 1500, and it retains some of the original features, such as the fireplace, beams and stonework. The inn kept the 'Chequers' name, inspired by the money-lender sign. In the mid-eighteenth century it housed a semi-permanent

Chequers Inn.

zoo of fourteen beasts, including a camel, a racoon, an opossum, a 'sea lioness' and 'a very large fish, possibly a shark'.

Legend speaks of an underground passage that links the Chequers with the Mitre pub over the road (a favourite of Doctor Samuel Johnson). Some monks were sealed in here in the 1530s and their dying shrieks and groans can still be heard. The complete absence of verifying data (i.e. no bones and no tunnel) should not deter you from having a listen.

In the late sixteenth century, Oxford landlord Matthew Harrison (1556–1630) kept a bear named Furze. The unorthodox pet is said to have inspired (or at least reinforced) the name of Harrison's premises, The Bear Inn. The pub was probably named after the city's adjacent bear baiting pit. Near Bear Lane, but actually on the equally narrow

Wheatsheaf Lane.

Alfred Street, The Bear is still a favourite drinking venue for students from Christ Church, Oriel and beyond, and is renowned for its collection of more than 4,500 cut-off ties. The original building was demolished in 1801: the present Bear Inn was formerly an ostler's house attached to the pub, which provided horses for travellers.

The Eagle and Child on St Giles is renowned as the favoured watering hole of fantasisers J.R.R. Tolkien and C.S. Lewis. It is known locally as The Bird and Baby.

Wheatsheaf Lane is a claustrophobic passageway off the High Street, leading to the characterful Wheatsheaf pub. It has netting overhead to prevent dead pigeons dropping on your head, and props that keep the buildings on either side from tumbling in drunken embrace. The Lane used to house Gill and Company, Britain's oldest ironmonger business, founded in 1530. It closed in 2010, victim of the recession.

Special mention must go to the snug Half Moon in St Clements, which hosts live music several nights a week, including the jewel in the crown, a long-standing Irish session on Sunday afternoons.

Indian taken away

The old Indian Institute on the corner of Catte Street and Holywell Street was established in 1884, its aim being 'the work of fostering and facilitating Indian studies in the university; the work of making Englishmen, and even Indians themselves, appreciate better than they have done before the languages, literature and industries of India'. There are tell-tell signs reminding us of the Indian connection, such as the elephant and howdah weathervane, as well as other external and internal details. The building is currently Oxford Martin School (originally called the James Martin 21st Century School)

Indian Institute building on May Morning. (Photograph by Heather Robbins)

which sets out 'to address the most pressing global challenges and opportunities of the 21st century.' It was founded by Dr James Martin, IT expert and author, who has probably given Oxford more money than any other single benefactor in its history.

Brief encounters

Old Headington, Old Marston and Headington Quarry are all intact, picturesque villages trapped behind the bland exterior of suburbia. Their charms are hidden from the main road, but worth seeking out.

A pair of beautiful golden **satyrs** prop up the lintel of a doorway on St Mary's Passage, off the High Street.

The **old mill at Osney Lock Marina**, visible from Mill Street as part of a new development of posh flats, was the last melancholy remnant of the once magnificent twelfth-century Osney Abbey. The 'Abbot of Osney Abbey' title still exists – it is held by a Catholic priest, in

Satyrs.

a role known as Titular Abbot. This odd breed hold the Abbot titles of the many suppressed, dissolved and destroyed monastic buildings of Britain.

Bulwarks' Lane, between New Street and George Street, has the original cobbles and gas lamps of a bygone age. You'll emerge into the shops and buses of frenetic Queen Street (known as Butcher Row prior to 1838) and reel from the shock of the twenty-first century.

St Frideswide's Church on Botley Road was built in the Gothic Revival era of the nineteenth century, an architectural whitewash that has not aged very well. This particular example has an odd stumpy charm, though, the strange proportion of tower to main building being the result of a project that ran out of money. The tower, last on the list of jobs to be done, was never completed.

Osney Abbey and its remains.

St Martin can be seen in traditional guise in a fresco over the archway in front of the café beside St Martin's tower at Carfax. The saint is chopping off a section of his cloak to give to a beggar – a scene that was supposed to have taken place in fourth-century Hungary when Martin, later a bishop, was still a mere kind-hearted soldier in the Roman army.

Bath Place is a beautiful corner of seventeenth-century wobbly houses and cobbles off Holywell Street. It was formerly known as Hell Passage, or (as in the 1772 Survey of Oxford) simply Hell. Its southern end crosses a parish boundary and is officially a separate lane, St Helen's Passage (probably a bowdlerisation of 'Hell').

The fresco at St Martin's.

An old **parish boundary stone** is captured behind glass in the unlikely setting of the ladies' department at Marks & Spencer's, just to the right of the row of tills.

Several **university college boathouses** can be seen where Christ Church Meadow meets the Thames. All the college boating clubs used to have grand barges, but they have now disappeared in favour of these more practical boathouses.

Boundary stone at Marks & Spencer's.

Designed by John Plowman and completed in 1841, **County Hall** on New Road was described by Charles Oman in *Castles* (1926) as 'quite the most abominable pseudo-Gothic Assize Court in all England', a label that goes some way towards making the ugly building more endearing.

Alderman John Parsons gave money in 1816 for the erection of **almshouses** in Kybald Street. They still survive, and have a stone plaque commemorating the deed, but were bought by University College in 1959. To compensate, the college had the new Parsons' Almshouses (designed by Thomas Rayson) built on the east side of Stone's Almshouses in St Clement's (originally a hospital, opened in 1700).

George Street, known these days for its theatre and multiple eateries, has a few relics from the past, including the **Corn Exchange** and **Old Fire Station** ('OFS' on the front of the building). Both were built between 1894 and 1896. The corn moved out in 1932, relocating (like the former Gloucester Green cattle market) to Oxpens, and the fire brigade moved to new premises on Rewley Road in 1971.

The castellated folly decorated with statues and cast iron balconies at **No. 5 Folly Bridge** (on a small island in the middle of the Thames) was built in 1849 for the mathematician Joshua Cardwell, possibly in homage to Friar Bacon's Study (the original 'folly' of Folly Bridge). It passed to another scientist, Robert Gunther, in 1911.

New College has a menagerie of carvings on its exterior walls. Surprising exhibits in this 1960s-carved corbel collection include aardvark, dung beetle, baboon, otter, harvest mouse, starfish, cassowary and crab, all visible from New College Lane.

No. 126 High Street (next door to Kemp Hall, mentioned on p.168) dates from the fourteenth century, a fact concealed by its beautiful seventeenth-century frontage, featuring original leaded windows.

Friar Bacon's study.

Across the road from No. 126, the three entrances to the **Covered Market** can be seen, aligned symmetrically beneath its unifying, grand stone façade – the original frontage of the market, oddly invisible in this age of big plate-glass shop window displays.

The south porch of **St Mary's Church** on the High has impressive but incongruous spiral columns, modelled on St Peter's Basilica in The Vatican. They were installed in 1637 under the guidance of University Chancellor William Laud (who got into far more trouble – beheaded, eventually – for his supposed 'popery' in erecting the attendant statue of the Virgin Mary). The church tower dates from the thirteenth century, with the spire plonked on top a hundred years later.

Off Pembroke Square, outside **Pembroke College Chapel**, bicycles, gravestones and tombs gather on the pavement or lean on the walls like youths waiting for something interesting to happen. Some of the paving stones here are former grave-markers too, the stoneware all ejected from the former chapel graveyard.

Pembroke College Chapel and old graveyard.

St Giles' church and yews.

The **church of St Giles** was originally built on the site of a pre-Christian temple and the oldest yew tree in the churchyard are said to predate the whole lot. Next to the churchyard is a lovely cast iron **sundial**, a gift from twin town Bonn, unveiled in 1985. Its only drawback is that it appears to be about thirty minutes fast or slow (depending on the time of year).

Non-mobile phones

The three red telephone boxes on Catte Street, Jowett Walk and Pembroke Street are Grade II listed, having survived the invasion of the 1980s boxes that replaced most of these 1920s and '30s models. All the other old red phone kiosks in Oxford have been moved to their current locations from elsewhere.

The Grade II listing has not prevented the Pembroke Street box from being drastically tampered with. The Toy

Museum has been having fun with it, giving it an *Owl and the Pussycat* theme, and it is no longer functioning as a phone box.

Postscript

Fourteen Victorian post boxes have managed to survive in Oxford, including one in the Covered Market which is a slim line model dating from 1889–1901. The one at No. 78 Banbury Road, outside the house Sunnyside, is an 'Anonymous box' lacking the words 'Post Office' and the royal initials. It was installed in 1885 specifically to serve the needs of Sir James Murray, who lived in the house and generated a colossal amount of correspondence from his garden 'Scriptorium', which is where the first *Oxford English Dictionary* was compiled.

The oldest of the boxes, an 1866 Hexagonal Penfold model, is on Park Town. There are also eight wall-mounted Victorian boxes inscribed W.T. Allen & Co. London, all installed in the 1880s with locations including Merton Street and Holywell Street.

Chapter Seven

Highlights of the Museums

The Ashmolean

Crown jewel

Alfred mec heht gewyrcan, 'Alfred had me made', declares the dragon-headed treasure known as the

Alfred Jewel. It is thought to have been created at the command of ninth-century King Alfred the Great, perhaps as the handle of a rod or small staff with which to point to lines in a book whilst reading (rather like Rabbis when reciting from the Torah). The Jewel was discovered in Somerset in 1693, and bequeathed to Oxford University by its first owner Colonel Nathaniel Palmer (1661–1718).

Ashmolean.

Indoor fireworks

The museum has Guy Fawkes's lantern. This was donated to the university in 1641 by Robert Heywood, the son of one of the Justices of the Peace who had apprehended the hapless Fawkes in the cellars of Parliament House on 5 November 1605.

Famous names

With drawings by Michelangelo, Raphael and Leonardo da Vinci – leaves from their sketchbooks, as intimate as diary entries – the art collection of The Ashmolean is wonderful, and it should suffice merely to drop further major-league names such as J.M.W. Turner, John Constable, Pablo Picasso, Paolo Uccello, Piero di Cosimo and Claude Lorraine.

King of the fiddles

The Messiah Stradivarius, by violin-maker Antonio Stradivari, is trapped behind glass away from the hands of violin players.

Deathly images

A death mask of Oliver Cromwell is on display, warts and all. It's not the only one in town, though, as the Museum of Oxford has one too. These are just two of the dozens that survived – clearly, a lot of people wanted to see Oliver dead.

Egypt

My children assure me that the Egyptian section of the museum has the real highlights, including the ram-headed Amon, the crocodile-headed Sobek, a good selection of mummies, some vivid coffin 'death mask' portraits, a cornucopia of clay models (including a mongoose that the kids are particularly fond of), and a bewildering array of scarab beetles.

Oxford University Museum of Natural History

The Oxford Dodo

The Dodo remains (originally in the Ashmolean Museum) are the ones that inspired the Dodo in Lewis Carroll's *Alice in Wonderland*. Tragically, the specimen – originally described as 'Dodar from the island Mauritius; it is not able to flie being so big' – was in such a sorry state by 1755 that the body was burnt, with just the head and feet preserved. The ravages of time, the carnivorous efforts of Dermestid beetles and the relatively primitive nature of contemporary taxidermy, were all to blame.

Hillaire Belloc, in his *Cautionary Verses* (1907) commemorated the Oxford Dodo:

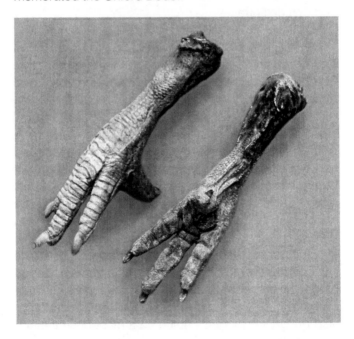

Dodo foot.

The voice which used to squawk and squeak
Is now for ever dumb –
Yet you may see his bones and beak
All in the Mu-se-um.

You may be disappointed to learn that the actual bits on display in the museum are casts, the original parts safely tucked away in store.

Oxford Dinosaurs

Amongst the many dinosaur bones in the museum are some Oxfordshire specialities. These include the following:

Megalosaurus ('huge lizard'), a carnivore from the Middle Jurassic, the grand matriarch of dinosaurs. Christ Church's William Buckland discovered specimens at Stonesfield, and the beast was named *Megalosaurus bucklandii*. In 1842, Richard Owen, professor of the Royal College of Surgeons in London, placed Megalosaurus in a new class of animals – the Dinosaurs.

Cetiosaurus oxoniensis, translating as 'Oxford whale lizard', was a brontosaurus-type beast. The first specimen appeared at Chipping Norton in 1825 and the remnants on display in the museum were discovered in 1860 by watch-maker Mr Chapman. He hopped off the train at Kirtlington Station as the Cetiosaurus remains were being shovelled to one side by oblivious workmen. Recognising a pile of monster bones when he saw one, Chapman telegraphed the museum's first curator, Professor of Geology John Phillips, who oversaw the bones' removal to the glass cases of Academia. In his enthusiasm, Phillips took all the credit.

The Jurassic *Eustreptospondylus oxoniensis,* 'Oxford well-turned vertebra', belonged to the family that spawned the more celebrated Tyrannosaurus rex. The museum's specimen is the most complete Carnosaur ever discovered in Europe. It was discovered in 1871 in a Summertown brick pit, the same pit from which many of the museum's own bricks were sourced.

The Tuna of death!

In 1846 Henry Wentworth Acland, Oxford University Lecturer in Anatomy, took his old tutor H.G. Liddell, Dean of Christ Church, on a winter sun-seeking trip to Madeira. Liddell – who was the father of Lewis Carroll's young heroine Alice – was in poor health, and the sea air around the island was meant to do him good. Unfortunately, the sea did not prove kind on the return journey.

The companions' steamship *Tyne* was caught in a storm off the Bay of Biscay on 12 January and struck a reef 1 mile off the Dorset coast. The passengers were all hauled to safety at dawn, and amongst the salvage, to Acland's relief, was a large Bluefin tuna that he had brought from Madeira. It had been packed in salt and interred in an 8ft-long box with the legend: 'Dr Acland, Oxford'. The crew of the *Tyne*, however, were not so happy to see the relic rescued.

Rumour had spread during the voyage, saying that the coffin-like box contained a corpse, probably one of Acland's patients. A storm at sea is the ideal breeding ground for superstition, and many people blamed the presence of the 'corpse' for the calamity. This was all in line with tradition, as any elemental mishap at sea is said to have its origin in some person or object on board.

At one point the crew had threatened mutiny, and the captain informed Acland that he intended to throw the ominous box overboard. Acland, desperate to retain his specimen, threatened legal proceedings. He made assurances that the oversized tin contained tuna, but no one would believe him.

There was nothing else for it. A metaphorical tin-opener was summoned, in the form of a carpenter with a screwdriver. Inside the box, of course, the assembled company

discovered a large fish. During the salvage, the embar-
rassed sailors made it their primary task to rescue the
'tunny', which was eventually delivered to the museum
at Christ Church unharmed. Later, the fish skeleton was
displayed in the Anatomy School, and was moved in 1860
to the University Museum of Natural History, where it can
still be seen today.

The original Latin inscription for the fish was rather dull,
given its exciting posthumous history. To remedy things,
Charles Dodgson – that man Lewis Carroll again – made
a line-for-line parody of the inscription. Thus the words,
'The tunny you are peering at exceeded all expectations',
became, 'The tunny you are sneering at exceeded even
Oxford's capacity for surprise', and so on.

Live specimens

For visitors who venture upstairs, there are a few living
exhibits hidden away. These include a bee colony and a
glass tank containing Madagascan hissing cockroaches.

The Pitt-Rivers Museum

For a concise tour of human life, death and beliefs, no
museum can match The Pitt-Rivers Museum. Opened in
1884, it looks like an extra-terrestrial's collection from his
hunting trip to earth during the early years of the twentieth century. All manner of human treasures can be found
here, no doubt meaningful to the people and place from
which they came, but all strangely meaningless when
bunched together in the gloomy labyrinthine interior of this
unique museum.

In this setting, the animal gods of Egyptians, the feath-
ered head dresses of Polynesians and the Morris trousers
of bricklayers from Headington all look oddly similar.
Cabinets of ceremonial dress and carvings of religious

significance are just cabinets of curiosities when seen in a single collection, out of context. But the experience is fascinating and provides a broad and highly entertaining overview of the eccentricities of our very singular species.

Most controversial of all are the human remains – bones, scalps and shrunken heads. Amazonian decapitees are still on display, looking like the *Dorian Grey* images of Victorian porcelain dolls; but the tattooed Maori heads were removed in 1987 after a quiet word from a visiting Maori dignitary.

In 1928 a red-streaked celt – a stone believed to be a thunderbolt – from Sangratsu in India's Naga Hills was sent to the Pitt Rivers Museum. Its native owner claimed that it was still 'live' and had caused much damage, including a lightning strike which had destroyed his house. He had picked it up as a good luck talisman, but was now keen to part with it.

The man who relieved him of the burden, Mr C.W. Pawsey, warned Dr Hutton at the museum that he had 'better dispose of the celt quickly, unless you want a new bungalow!' It was duly installed, but was still fizzing. In November 1928 a great storm blew away a large portion of the Pitt-Rivers roof, and only the cold logic of a scientist would claim that the cause was anything other than the stone thunderbolt from the stormy Naga Hills.

Chapter Eight

Oxford Specialities: What's in a Name?

Deciding to sell jars of his wife's marmalade from his shop at No. 84 High Street in 1874 was Frank Cooper's master stroke. As soon as Oxford dons and students acquired the taste for it, lured by the 'Oxford Marmalade' tag, its fame was sealed. In those days Oxford supplied most of the high ranking jobs in the Empire, and wherever Oxfordians went the marmalade went with them.

Cooper's opened a purpose-built factory in 1900 on the corner of Hollybush Row and Park End Street. The unthinkable happened when the company was acquired by Premier Foods in 1967, moving production out of Oxford and leaving its former premises, the Jam factory (currently a restaurant and arts venue) unpreserved.

Cooper's Marmalade accompanied Scott to the Antarctic, and real and imaginary fans include the Queen and James Bond.

Several other products, materials or items of clothing are known as 'oxford' or 'oxfords'.

The Secret History of Oxford

Oxford accent   a local take on Received Pronunciation and the now extinct 'BBC accent'.

Oxford Blue   the official blue used by the university (aka Pantone 282 or hex code #002147). Strictly speaking it is a tone of azure. Oxford Blues is also the name of official university sport teams.

Oxford Blue, Oxford Isis and College White   some of the cheeses produced by the Oxford Cheese Company. They have a stall at the Indoor Market.

Oxford Brown   the classic, brown farmyard chicken.

Oxford   Cockney rhyming slang for 'face', short for 'Oxford and Cambridge Boat Race', more commonly 'boat' as in 'he had an Oxford/boat like a bunch of kippers'.

Oxford Clay   fossil-filled clays from the Oxfordian age of the Late Jurassic epoch, around 160 million years old.

Oxford Down   sheep breed, first appeared in the 1830s after crossing Cotswold rams with Hampshire Down and Southdown ewes.

Oxford English   as well as being another form of 'Oxford accent', the term also refers to the *Oxford English Dictionary*'s language research programme database, which includes English quotations and examples from a wide range of media, featuring over two billion words.

Oxford Items: What's in a Name?

Oxford Lamb — sometimes called Oxford John, a dish of seasoned lamb or mutton, sliced thinly.

Oxford Ochre — yellow ochre (a naturally occurring iron oxide clay) formerly mined in bulk at Shotover.

Oxford Oolite — coarse-grained limestone, aka 'Oxfordian'.

Oxford Pillowcase — the ones with a 'frame' of material around them, which supposedly stiffens the bag.

Oxford Punch — as in the alcoholic drink, the 'Oxford' has dissolved cow's foot jelly in it. Not in huge demand these days, funnily enough.

Oxford Ragwort (*Senecio squalidus*) — escaped from the Botanic Gardens in the eighteenth century, spreading rapidly due to its ability to colonise wasteland such as railway sidings.

Oxford Sauce — an ancient recipe based on Cumberland sauce. Since 2000 'Baron Pouget's Oxford Sauce' has been available, bearing little resemblance to the former.

Oxford Sandy and Black — breed of pig, not unrelated to the following...

Oxford Sausage — recipe open to discussion, but often featuring sage and lemon.

Oxford Scholar — Australian and Cockney rhyming slang for 'dollar'.

Oxford Shirts — cotton or cotton mix, known as 'Oxford cloth', usually manifesting as sober and smart white, striped, or 'Oxford grey'.

Oxford Shoes — leather, with 'closed lacing' eyelets stitched underneath the top 'vamp' part of the shoe, rather than on top.

Oxford Time — five minutes later than Greenwich Mean Time, the reason being that noon in Oxford occurs five minutes (and two seconds) later than noon in Greenwich.

Oxford Trousers — 'Oxford bags' were the original baggy trousers, popular with students in the 1920s, revived in the 1970s and still to be seen flapping in a stiff Thames Valley wind.

Oxford University Press — the original university printing house, first located in the Clarendon Building and currently on Walton Street.

Oxford Weed (*Cymbalaria murali*) — Ivy-leaved toadflax, a native of Italy that followed Oxford ragwort's example.

Oxford University Press building.

Oxforth Symphony?

The most famous piece of music associated with the city is probably Joseph Haydn's *Oxford Symphony*. In 1791 the mightily prolific composer became an honorary Doctor of Music at Oxford University. To mark the occasion he conducted a performance of his *Symphony No. 92 in G major*, thereafter known as the *Oxford Symphony* (it being part of the agreement that receipt of the doctorate would involve him conducting three of his works).

Conjuring dazzling images of bright Cotswold stone, energetic students and beautiful, sweeping, majestic academia, the whole notion is undermined a bit by the fact that it wasn't actually written with Oxford in mind at all. Haydn had first conducted the work in Paris some time earlier. He had not yet started work on his portfolio of 'English' pieces (the twelve *London Symphonies*), and so for the event in Oxford he simply led with his latest big hit.

Many of the musicians in the Oxford performance were already familiar with the work, which was very handy with no time for rehearsal. Haydn was a little cynical, writing to a friend: 'I had to pay one and a half guineas for the bell peals at Oxforth when I received the doctor's degree, and half a guinea for the robe.'

Oxford Coffee

Coffee was first sold in Oxfordshire in 1650, when a man called Jacob began supplying it in St Peter-in-the-East parish in Oxford. It was said to have been imbibed by those 'who delight in novelty' and, according to seventeenth-century Oxford Historian Anthony Wood, 'others who esteemed themselves either Virtuosi or Wits'.

Nathanael Konopios of Crete was the man who actually introduced the beverage to the city, though.

He was living at Balliol College, having been sent by Greek Orthodox Church Patriarch Cyril Loukaris in the 1630s as part of his attempt to find common ground with Protestant nations. The religious mission was a failure, but coffee worship has never left the city. Queen's Lane Coffee House (recently rebranded as QL) was founded in 1654 and is still operating as a coffee shop. The Grand Café over the road claims to be an even older coffee emporium, basing its antiquity on a mention by Samuel Pepys in 1650.

Coffee consumption was boosted by the fact that it was taxed at a lower rate than the other up-and-coming tipples chocolate and tea (known as 'catlap' and dismissed as a woman's brew by chauvinistic coffee drinkers).

The Oxford Movement

The 'Tractarians' who provided the philosophical and spiritual rudders for the Oxford Movement, were university academics-cum-clergy who were concerned that the surge of liberal social reform that defined nineteenth-century English politics would lead to the withdrawal of state support for the Church of England. They looked for a new way of instilling meaningful vigour to religious proceedings. Rather than following the low church trend of nonconformists, they looked to the pre-Reformation medieval English church for inspiration. This involved lots of ritual and mysticism, and eventually led the Oxford Movement to go the final mile and embrace Roman Catholicism.

The Museum Swifts

There are surely no swifts as famous or as scrutinized as the ones that make their home in the tower at Oxford's University Museum of Natural History. Observations in and around the tower's ventilation shafts – where up to 147 pairs reside – have been ongoing since 1948 when David Lack, head of the Edward Grey Institute at the Department of Zoology, established The Oxford Swift Research Project. It is one of the longest continuous studies of a single bird species in the world. There is a dedicated book on the subject, *Swifts in a Tower*, the first edition of which appeared in 1956. These days we can all join in – there is a Webcam installed, and images are relayed to a monitor in the museum, or can be ogled at on the museum's website at www.oum.ox.ac.uk/swifts.

Deer in the Grove

Magdalen's herd of fallow deer shakes its antlers in surroundings which belong more to country park than bustling metropolis. They have been resident in The Grove deer park for 300 years or so. The beasts are culled to control numbers (usually in December, to the benefit of the butchers of Oxford's Covered Market) and are eaten on special college occasions.

The deer do not graze here in spring, during the flowering and seeding season of local botanical speciality the Snakeshead fritillary (*Fritillaria meleagris*), a formerly common plant that was harvested mercilessly for sale at the Oxford market. For July and August the deer are relocated to Magdalen Meadow to crop the grass after the fritillary has set its seed. They are herded back to The Grove in December (unaware of their possible tryst with the college guns).

Formerly the herd was limited to forty, this being the number of scholars according to the College's Constitution. Herds are allowed to be larger these days, following good management and stringent veterinary monitoring. However, in 1939 the deer nearly found a new master when the Ministry of Food became responsible for all meat production in the UK. The Magdalen dons argued that their beasts were not meat, but, owing to their vital grass-cropping role, part of the vegetation of The Grove. By this convoluted logic they evaded the Ministry.

The deer, when culling time is upon them, are shot by marksmen from inside the college to prevent the animals from associating the appearance of gunmen – and, by inference, all human visitors – with exploding gun-barrels and death. This used to come as a shock to students living on the ground floor of New Buildings – a favourite shooting spot – to which the deer stray very close. Since 1993, following a Junior Common Room petition, the deer are no longer culled in term time.

The Oxford Philosophical Club, AKA The Royal Society

In 1649 the inaugural meetings of the Oxford Philosophical Club, the precursor of the Royal Society (which still acts as chief scientific advisor to the British Government) took place at Wadham College. Key members of the Society's Oxford phase included architect Christopher Wren; proto-neurologist and doctor of anatomy Thomas Willis; pre-eminent scientist and jack-of-all-trades Robert Hooke; and Robert Boyle, one of the fathers of modern chemistry. On the wall of University College, marking the site of Cross Hall (one of the many lost university halls) where the two men did much of their work, is an inscription, reading:

In a house on this site between 1655 and 1668 lived ROBERT BOYLE. Here he discovered BOYLE'S LAW and made experiments with an AIR PUMP designed by his assistant ROBERT HOOKE Inventor Scientist and Architect who made a MICROSCOPE and thereby first identified the LIVING CELL.

The Oxford–Cambridge Cricket Match

The first cricket match between Oxford and Cambridge took place in 1827, the oldest first class fixture in the world. Cricket was being played in Oxford as early as 1729, and Samuel Johnson recalled playing whilst studying at Pembroke College.

The Oxford–Cambridge Boat Race

The Oxford-Cambridge Boat Race takes place every April on a stretch of the River Thames. First raced in 1829, it now attracts up to 250,000 spectators plus millions of TV viewers. After all these years it is a closely run thing, with Cambridge maintaining a narrow lead. It is said that each member of the team trains for two hours for every stroke in the race, and it takes an average 600 strokes to get to the finishing line.

The Thames/Isis

The Thames' alternative name in Oxford is the Isis, usually applied only to that section that flows through the city. The distinction is little more than affectation and comes from a simple separation of the syllables in the Romano-British name for the river, Tamesis. The name is still used by the Ordnance Survey for the whole stretch between Oxford and Dorchester-on-Thames.

The Treacle Well

St Margaret's well in the churchyard at Binsey is known colloquially as the Treacle Well. This title used to denote nothing more than a curative well (treacle being a word for a healing balm or liquid), but Lewis Carroll found the name irresistible and used it as the basis for the Treacle Well in *Alice in Wonderland*. As the Mad Hatter says: 'You can draw water out of a water-well, so I should think you could draw treacle out of a treacle well – eh, stupid?'

The Boar's Head Legend and Feast

St Giles Church in Horspath near Oxford has a seventeenth-century stained glass depiction of John Copcot putting a book into the mouth of a wild boar. This commemorates a legend in which fifteenth-century student Copcot of Queen's College, was walking through nearby Shotover Forest reading Aristotle. Surprised by an angry boar, he used the only weapon available – the book. He thrust it down the beast's throat with the words *Graecum est* – it's all Greek to me. In other versions it is the expiring pig that utters the immortal words.

Copcot took the beast's head back to Queen's College in Oxford, which marks the occasion every year near Christmas with the private Boar's Head Ceremony. The centrepiece is a cooked boar's head, crowned and garlanded with laurel, bay, mistletoe, rosemary and small heraldic flags. At the entry of this delicacy, 'The Boar's Head Carol' is sung, the earliest versions of which date from the fifteenth-century. The song was recorded, Latin refrains and all, as a not-very-hit single by Steeleye Span in 1978.

St Giles Fair

The annual St Giles Fair is a standard funfair these days. But in the past it boasted all manner of entertainments, from theatres and exhibitions to zoos and circuses. This local newspaper excerpt from 1819 gives a little flavour of the long forgotten fun of the fair.

Oxford Items: What's in a Name?

Madame Louis Colombier's truly elegant DEVICES in EQUILIBRIUMS; Mr Gyngell will introduce several AIRS on a complete Treble Set of MUSICAL GLASSES; a Grand Hydraulical Exhibition of FIRE, and WATER; Mons. Rene Colombier will DANCE A HORNPIPE ON HIS HEAD; Monsieur Louis Colombier will DANCE A HORNPIPE BLINDFOLDED, AMONGST NINE REAL EGGS; Mr GYNGELL's unequalled OLYMPIC EXERCISES... the FEMALE ITALIAN HERCULES, who is allowed to be the strongest Woman in the world, with her Hair. She will, amongst various feats of unparalleled strength, lift Eight Hundred Weight by the HAIR of her HEAD! which she will challenge any man or woman in England for 100 Guineas to do the like... Also, Signora VALENTINI, daughter of the Female Hercules, only 14 years of age, will perform several astonishing FEATS OF STRENGTH! She will lift a Table with her Teeth and two persons upon it... The celebrated, grand, and unrivalled TYROLESIAN PEASANTS' DANCE, ON STILTS FOUR FEET HIGH! with an Allemande, Waltz, Quadrille, and sing their German Melody. Admission – Front seats, 1s. – Back seats 6d.

In 1863 'a Kaffir, who ate rats in a raw state, attracted some curiosity – and disgust.' Offended sensibilities were not the only risks that fair-goers took. Oxford City Council was at pains to warn people of the four great dangers of the fair – drunkenness, theft, cholera and gangs of over-excited youths. The first of these problems was attacked via printed horror stories detailing the evils of alcohol, plus stalls manned by the Temperence (teetotal) movement.

Cholera warnings from the Oxford Board of Health claimed that the disease could be caused by 'immoderate drinking', 'eating unripe fruits' and 'being out late at night, and from all excess, and immoral indulgence'. They concluded 'In consequence of the Cholera having visited this City, the authorities have given orders that the Fair shall be confined within the narrowest limits allowed by law'.

In 1879 the Mayor ordered 'whips and other devices' to be confiscated. But pranksters found 'a worse nuisance...the deliberate throwing of handfuls of flour, bran, rice and sawdust into the faces of promenaders'. In 1880 they added Cayenne pepper to their artillery. And if weapons failed, there was always a more direct approach. In 1888 the newspaper reported: 'Some young men exhibited their vulgarity and want of propriety by dashing here and there and unceremoniously kissing any and every young woman they met, and in some instances they were met with a very proper rebuff for the outrageous liberty they took.'

Other Fairs

St Giles Fair still takes place on the first weekend after 1 September (St Giles Day). It is at least 300 years old, probably much older, although its exact origins are unknown. Oxford used to have other fairs, including one at Lower Wolvercote, which disappeared in the fifteenth century. The Great Fair of St Frideswide took place annually in what is now Christ Church Meadow, until the college was founded in the sixteenth century. Gloucester Green Fair was another annual event, based at the old cattle market (currently the market place and bus station). The fair ceased in the nineteenth century, but the site maintains the old tradition, hosting events such as Oxford's annual Green Market and Antiques Fair. St Clement's was Oxford's second biggest fair after St Giles, but this too came to an end in the nineteenth century, plagued by good old-fashioned robbery and debauchery.

Christ Church Meadow's roe deer and mistletoe. The fair was once held here.

Oxfam

The embryonic Oxford Committee for Famine Relief held its first public meeting in the library of the Church of St Mary the Virgin in Oxford in 1942. The organisers, all like-minded Quakers, were concerned that the British Government's policy of preventing the importation of food supplies into German-controlled mainland Europe was causing hardship to the oppressed civilians. The Oxford Committee, along with others throughout Britain, urged the government to allow controlled distribution to civilians under the guiding hand of the International Red Cross, their specific concern being the people of occupied Greece, known to be dying in their thousands through starvation.

After the war, as Oxfam, the Committee continued to organise collections of food and clothing when all the other wartime organisations had folded. By the late 1950s Oxfam was active in most of the poorer parts of the world. The headquarters of Oxfam GB are still in Oxford, at Cowley, and it employs more than 6,000 people worldwide. There is a Blue Plaque commemorating founder and first Honorary Secretary Cecil Jackson-Cole (1901–79) at No. 17 Broad Street.

Oxford Gas

Oxford has several surviving gas lamps (all fitted with bulbs now), the precursors of electric street lights. The city's gaslight system was ignited in 1819 and examples of the old lampposts can be seen throughout the city, notably on the High Street, Radcliffe Square, Brasenose Lane, Merton Street and many of the adjacent thoroughfares.

Oxford used to be renowned for the quality of its gas. Writing in 1828, Nathaniel Whittock enthused:

> The gas produced here is remarkably pure and brilliant; and by the judicious and liberal arrangement of the laws of the company, the lighting of the city in every part is considered of more importance than the accumulation of profit to the individuals; consequently the illumination of the city, during the winter months, is as brilliant as can be desired.

Mistletoe

The city has a huge amount of mistletoe in its many parks and green areas, often mistaken for the nests of crows or magpies. Particularly impressive globes of the parasitic love-weed can be seen in Christ Church Meadow, Magdalen meadows, the Botanic Gardens and Parks Road.

Gaslight on Merton Street. (Photograph by Jan Sullivan)

The Quarter Boys

The two figures who strike the small bell on the wall of St Martin's at Carfax every quarter of an hour are the Quarter Boys. The current pair, refurbished in 2013, was set up in the eighteenth century, replacing the Tudor originals (which are in the keeping of the Museum of Oxford in the Town Hall on St Aldates). One of the Boys fell from his perch in the early 1800s, and an advert appeared in the local newspaper, purporting to be from Oxford academic Dickey James, who was famous for his short stature. The advert announced that Dr James 'intended offering himself as a replacement for the fallen Quarter Boy.'

The Quarter Boys.

Oxford Lingo

It's a linguistic quagmire out there on the Oxford streets. Here's a brief list to sort your Battells from your formals:

Oxford Items: What's in a Name?

Batells	college bills
Bird and Baby	the Eagle and Child pub
Bod, the	Bodleian
Bops	college discos
Broad, the	Broad Street
Bumping races	dodgems-style races on the narrow river
Chair	an academic post
Come up	to newly arrive at the Uni
Commoner	an undergraduate without a scholarship
Crew dates	mixed-sex groups meeting for a formal meal
DPhil	Doctor of Philosophy, Oxford's version of the PhD qualification
Duke Humphry's Guests	(archaic) students who work through the lunch hour, or can't afford lunch, named after the original bookworms of Duke Humphry's Library, the forerunner of the Bodleian. The hungry swots are said to be 'dining with Duke Humphry'
Eight	eight-oared rowing boat, used in Eights Week
Encaenia	ceremony handing out university Honours degrees, formerly in St Mary's Church, now in the Sheldonian Theatre
Entz	college entertainments

The Secret History of Oxford

Formals	college meals where diners wear fomal attire or gowns
Gated	confined to college as punishment
Gown	of the university (as opposed to 'Town')
Gaudy	reunion banquet at colleges
Great Tom	former monastic bell at Christ Church
Hearty	a keen sportsman
High, The	High Street
Highers	postgraduate degrees
Hilary	the spring term
Isis	alternative name for the Thames in Oxford
Island	the Osney district of Oxford
Maudlin	how 'Magdalen' is pronounced
Michealmas	the autumn term
MPhil	Master of Philosophy, Oxford's version of the MA qualification
OED	Oxford English Dictionary
Other Place, the	Cambridge (or, tongue in cheek, Oxford Brookes University)
OUP	Oxford University Press
Oxfordian	an Oxford resident
Oxonian	an Oxford graduate
Plodge	Porter's Lodge
Plough	to fail an exam
Porters	guard-like lodge keepers/postmasters/college security men, etc.

Oxford Items: What's in a Name?

Proctors	a kind of college police force
Quad	college quadrangles
Quarry	Headington Quarry district, also the name of a celebrated Morris side
Regius Professor	one appointed by the crown
Rustication	temporarily removed from the university
Sconce	to demand a forfeit for offence against table etiquette (see p.239)
Scout	the person who cleans the rooms and empties the college bins
Sent down	forced to leave the university
Sporting the oak	closing a door to signify 'do not disturb'
Subfusc	formal dress for exams
Taylorian, Taylor, Tay-Tay	the Taylor Institution building on St Giles
Trinity	third term of academic year; also the name of a college
Turl, the	Turl Street
Union Society	the university's famous debating society
Univ	frequently used name for University College
Up	the route to Oxford, from anywhere
Vac	university vacations, e.g. Long

Chapter Nine

Oxford
Curiosities

This A-Z selection gives a time-spanning taster of unorthodox Oxford.

Aurochs

Queens College has a ceremonial 'loving cup' donated by founder Robert Eglesfield. It is made from the horn of an aurochs (pronounced our-ox), the extinct wild cow whose name is the origin of the word 'ox'. A very appropriate token for a college in the city of Ox-ford.

Bathing, al fresco

Parson's Pleasure (originally Patten's Pleasure) in the University Parks at Oxford was the city's concession to naturism. Closed in the 1990s, for centuries this section of the River Cherwell had been the place where gentlemen of the university would get their kit off and take a dip. Anthony Wood, the seventeenth-century city historian, records that a student once drowned there. Warden of All Souls John Sparrow once refused to conceal his identity (unlike the rest of his skinny-dipping party) when a gaggle of girls came sailing by. In defence of his over exposure, Sparrow proclaimed, 'I don't know about you, but most people recognise me by my face!'

The city's other official riverside bathing spots included Dames Delight, a spot for women and children further along the river in the Parks. Tumbling Bay is still frequented for al fresco dips, behind the Botley Road allotments. These days the justifiably popular outdoor bathing pool at Hinksey does its bit to fill the gap.

Bear

Frank Buckland (1826–80) kept large numbers of animals, living and dead, at his home in Christ Church College. His personal favourite was a black bear named Tiglath-pileser – Tig for short – who 'walked round your chair and rasped your hand with treelike tongue', as recalled by family friend William Tuckwell. Regarding the name, Tuckwell continues:

> On a certain morning in May the bear escaped from Buckland's yard, and found his way into the chapel, at the moment when a student was reading the first lesson, 2 Kings xvi, and had reached the point at which King Ahaz was on his way to meet Tiglath-pileser, King of Assyria, at Damascus. The bear made straight for the Lectern, its occupant fled to his place, and the half-uttered name on his lips was transferred to the intruder.

Christ Church students sometimes dressed Tig in cap and gown for parties, or for boating trips with Buckland. Children would gather to marvel at the unorthodox regatta, much to the annoyance of Buckland. 'If threats failed [to move the children]', says Buckland's biographer George

Bompas, 'the bear was turned loose and shambled after them, whereupon they fled.'

Tig was present at the 1847 meeting of the British Association. One of the delegates, Moncton Milnes (later Lord Houghton), attempted to mesmerize the bear, which, according to Bompas, 'made Tig furious but he gradually yielded to the influence and at last fell senseless to the ground.'

At a time when dogs had been banned from the colleges, however, bears were never going to escape disapproving scrutiny. 'Mr Buckland', wrote the Dean of Christ Church after Tig's fame had gone before him, 'I hear you keep a bear in college; well, either you or your bear must go.' The bear, along with Frank Buckland's jackal Jacko and a pet eagle, were relocated to the Bucklands' estate in Islip, north-east of Oxford. Here the bear swapped a boat for a steed, happily riding on horseback.

The Islip idyll came to an end when Tig ram-raided a sweet shop. Bursting through the door, he clambered behind the counter and devoured the stock. The shopkeeper barricaded herself into the back room and sent someone out to summon help. Tig was hauled away, but returned on a number of other occasions, his addiction to sweets pointing the road to destruction.

Buckland, fed up of forking out to feed the bear's insatiable appetite, packed the contrite Tiglath-pileser off to London Zoo in 1847, where he died soon afterwards following an unsuccessful attempt to deal with his sugar-rotted teeth.

Beating the Bounds

In May each year the parish of St Michael at Northgate in Oxford Beats the Bounds. This once widespread tradition of marking parish boundaries has survived here in spite of physical obstacles. In fact it is the obstacles that make it so much fun, and which lure visitors from across the world to witness it.

Armed with willow wands, the bounds-beaters walk the traditional circuit, banging their sticks at each boundary stone with the cry 'Mark! Mark! Mark!' This seems particularly appropriate at one of the stones, which sits behind glass in Marks & Spencer's on Queen Street, marking the juncture of three parishes. There are halts in two other shops, a pub and the Town Hall. A section of old city wall is scaled, the university cathedral is beaten, and the final flagellation is in the grounds of Oriel College. Hot pennies are then thrown from the roof of Lincoln College down into the Quad for the children to scramble over while the grown-ups sip ground-ivy beer. Small penny-scramblers should be thankful that the rules have changed – in the old days the accompanying choirboys were beaten, not the stones, to encourage them to remember the boundaries.

Beer

All colleges used to produce their own beer and sing its praises. Brasenose still churns out Ale Verses each Shrove Tuesday, extolling the virtues of the brew, even though it is no longer produced on site.

Brasenose and Lincoln are conjoined colleges. The door that links them is seldom opened, but at lunchtime on Ascension Day (the day after the annual Beating of the Bounds ceremony) the door is flung wide and members of Brasenose are entitled to demand free ground-ivy beer from Lincoln. Like many of the best traditions, the origins of the free ground-ivy beer dole are disputed. One theory points to a Brasenose man who appealed to Lincoln for sanctuary after being chased by a murderous mob. Lincoln failed to unlock, and the man was bludgeoned to death before its gates. A rival story claims that a Lincoln man killed a Brasenose man in a duel. In both stories the penance was a beer dole. The ground ivy is said to have been introduced to spoil the drink and discourage Brasenose students from overindulging on hospitality. In reality, ground ivy is one of many additives that were used in beer-making before the universal availability of hops.

It is said that the conjoined walls of Brasenose and Lincoln were designed to enable drunken academics to pass from one college gate to the other without having to lose the support of the wall. A mutual drinking club used to fuddle the wits of the men on a weekly basis, the colleges taking it in turn to host the debaucheries. Sometimes the inebriates would stagger off course and end up in the middle of Radcliffe Square. There were no railings around the Radcliffe Camera in its early years, and the men, finding the safety of its wall, would assume they were back on track, and proceed to go round in circles all night like sodden goldfish. This, says folklore, is why the iron railings were erected: to keep out college drunks.

Radcliffe Square.

Bees

Robert Plot, first keeper of The Ashmolean in 1683, was one of the many commentators to describe the bee colony at Corpus Christi College, whose destruction in the Civil War almost forty years earlier was still being mourned as a local tragedy.

Bees were first brought to the college by Juan Luis Vives, aka Ludovicus Vives, who had been installed in 1520 as Professor of Rhetoric. However, it appears that the bees chose Vives, rather than the other way round: Plot says he 'was welcomed thither by a Swarm of Bees, which to signify the incomparable Sweetness of his Eloquence, settled themselves over his Head under the Leads of his Study (at the West-end of the cloister) where they continued about 130 Years.' This earned Corpus Christi the nickname the College of Bees.

Plot is happy to support the popular belief that bees react to the human events around them. When the president's Garden colony dispersed in 1648, it was because they supported the defeated Royalists of Charles I in the English Civil War. A smaller colony took over a corner of the college cloisters, but Plot says this did not include any of the original Vives-derived Royalist bees, and it dispersed soon after the Restoration of Charles II. Plot thinks it a great pity that Corpus Christi should no longer have 'the thing whereof their whole House is but the metaphor'.

Brasenose/brass nose

A gang of revolting students upped sticks from Brasenose in 1334, and settled in academic Stamford, Lincolnshire. As a souvenir they took with them the famous brass door-knocker from the college, an artefact shaped like a lion's head with a large ring through its nose. A few years later King Edward III ordered the students to return, but they left their knocker on Stamford's Brasenose Hall and there it remained until the 1890s. Stamford stayed in the academic doghouse, however – until the early nineteenth century, all Oxonians embarking on a Masters course at the university had to swear 'not to lecture in Stamford'.

The hall at Brasenose sports a collection of brass noses that have been attached to the college doors through the centuries. They are displayed in a glass case in the hall, with other examples for the nosey-at-heart in the college archives, including a nose tie-pin from the 1870s, and some nose-shaped tobacco pipes.

Bread Riots

In 1867 Oxford residents took umbrage at the price of bread. They had learned that the university was getting its loaves at a knock-down price from the city's main seller, the aptly named Isaac Grubb, one-time Mayor of Oxford. His windows were broken, and thousands took to the streets.

On 15 November 1867 *The Daily Telegraph* waxed purple: 'Oxford in tumult and riotous confusion! Her stately streets crowded with angry and starving people, her colleges shut up, and two companies of Granadier Guards, with forty pounds of ammunition per man, bivouacked in her Corn Exchange! Such a spectacle has scarcely been witnessed since the days when Rupert's Cavaliers clattered through The High.'

Bread riots!

Canals

The arrival of the canal system in the eighteenth century brought relief, and traffic (primarily coal) to a city prone not just to flooding, but to drying up. In the seventeenth century, historian Robert Plot wrote: 'The River Thames is not made so perfectly navigable to Oxford, but that in dry times, barges do sometimes lie aground three weeks, or a month, or more.'

The Oxford Canal was constructed to link London to the industrial Midlands, and the final stretch to Oxford was completed in 1790. For all its ingenious beauty, much of the Canal was built as cheaply as possible: single gates on the locks instead of double ones, lift or swing-bridges instead of sturdier, more expensive brick ones, the use of the existing stretches of the River Cherwell, and constructing twists and turns to get round hills (a so-called 'contour canal') rather than getting engineers to employ tunnel or aqueduct. Some of these contours were ironed out in the 1820s, but many remain.

The Oxford Canal's heyday was brief. Between 1790 and 1805 it carried all water traffic between London and the Midlands. But then the Grand Junction Canal opened, and much of the London traffic chose this new, more direct route. The one section that remained busy was between Napton and Braunston, which formed a link between the Warwick and Napton Canal and the Grand Junction. The Oxford Canal company had opposed the new canal, of course, and the Act which allowed the competition to go ahead included a clause by which Grand Junction paid Oxford 'bar tolls' as a form of compensation for the loss of traffic.

Horses were used on the Oxford Canal long after animal brawn had been superseded by coal and diesel. The last beast-powered barge retired in 1959. It had been pulled by a mule and was the last of Britain's horse-drawn freight narrowboats.

Cathedral and chapel

The head of Christ Church College is a Church of England Dean, and the college chapel doubles as Oxford's Cathedral (the smallest cathedral in the country), HQ of the Diocese of Oxford. It is, not surprisingly, the only college chapel in the world to lead a double life as a national cathedral. Paradoxically, it is not the university's official church – that honour goes to St Mary's on the High Street.

Crocodile

Frank Buckland (1826–1880) recalled riding, as a child, on a dying crocodile in the Quad at Christ Church. It had been brought from Southampton in the boot of a horse-drawn carriage in a 'semi-dead' state (according to Buckland's memoirs) and Frank's father, the eccentric lecturer and Dean William Buckland, had attempted to revive it in the fountain. It was served at the dining table over the following few days and is the last ingredient mentioned in this colourful recollection, by R. Tuckwell, of the carnivorous eccentricities of the household:

> A horse belonging to his brother-in-law, having been shot, Dr Buckland had the tongue pickled and served up at a large luncheon party, and the guests enjoyed it much, until told what they had eaten. Alligator was a rare delicacy, but puppies were occasionally, and mice frequently, eaten. So also at the Deanery, hedgehogs, tortoise, potted ostrich, and occasionally rats, frogs, and snails, were served up for the delectation of favoured guests. 'Party at the Deanery,' one guest notes, 'tripe for dinner; don't like crocodile for breakfast'.

Curse of Saint Frideswide

The first recorded death in Oxford appears in a chronicle for the year AD 924: 'This year King Edward died among the Mercians at Farndon; and very shortly, about sixteen days after this, Elward his son died at Oxford; and their bodies lie at Winchester.' This was the beginning of a long association between Oxford and royalty; and perhaps the first rumblings of the Curse of St Frideswide.

Oxford's patron saint Frideswide was born around 665 AD, and developed a fear and hatred of men. In what came to be known as the Curse of St Frideswide, it was said that no king who entered Oxford with violent intent would ever prosper.

When Harold Harefoot, who reigned over much of England between 1035 and 1040, died in the city after being 'elf-struck' while preparing his army for battle against his invading brother Harthacnut, superstitious heads nodded wisely.

In 1065 King Harold II parleyed with Northumbrian rebels in Oxford. The latter were defeated by the former at Stamford Bridge the following year; then poor Harold was famously skewered through the eye at the Battle of Hastings.

In 1263 Henry III, son of the luckless King John (who had been born in Oxford) entered the city with an army. Five years earlier the leading barons of England, led by Oxford hero Simon de Montfort, had forced the king to sign the Provisions of Oxford, by which the absolute monarchy of the Norman kings was brought to an end. Henry had managed to persuade the Pope to annul the Provisions in 1262. Aware of the Frideswide curse, the King wanted to prove that he, as divinely appointed ruler of England, was above such superstitious nonsense. He rallied his army here, with his son Edward in charge; but they were defeated at the Battle of Lewes soon after, and Henry was imprisoned by rebellious de Montfort. He should have remained superstitious.

Edward I, Henry's son, returned to Oxford in 1275. He rode as far as the East Gate of the city, and then turned back and lodged outside the city, to avoid the famous curse. This pragmatic move served him well – Edward went on to bring death and misery to most of Wales and Scotland, not to mention England's Jewish population, which was forcibly expelled 1290.

Charles I commandeered Oxford during the Civil War in 1645, and should have known better. Defeated and beheaded, he is the ultimate symbol of the curse.

Discipline (lack of)

In the eighteenth century academic Oxford was at low ebb, and discipline was lax. Edward Gibbon, historian, who went to Magdalen in 1752 at the age of fifteen, commented: 'The want of experience, of advice, and of occupation soon betrayed me into some improprieties of conduct, ill-chosen company, late hours, and inconsiderate expense... My frequent absence was visible and scandalous... without once feeling the hand of control... folly as well as vice should have awakened the attention of my superiors, and my tender years would have justified a more than ordinary degree of restraint and discipline.'

Lord Malmsbury was unimpressed too: 'The two years of my life I look back to as the most unprofitably spent were those I passed at Merton (1763–5). The discipline of the university happened at this particular moment to be so lax that a gentleman commoner was under no restraint, and never called on to attend lectures, chapel or hall. My tutor … gave himself no concern about his pupils. [We drank] claret, and we had our regular round of evening-card parties, to the great annoyance of our finances.'

Balliol student and poet Robert Southey, while accepting the pointlessness of it all, looked on the bright side of his years at the university (at the very end of the eighteenth century): 'There were but two things I learnt in Oxford – to row and to swim.'

Dragons

According to legend, in the first century AD King Lud was informed that two destructive brawling dragons would converge on the exact centre of the island – Oxford. Lud came to the city and dug a pit. At its base he placed a bowl of mead, covering it with a silk sheet. The dragons found the mead, drank it and got tangled up in the silk. Safely wrapped in their drunken stupor, they were carted off and buried under Mount Snowdon, where Merlin allegedly unearthed them 500 years later.

In the early 1700s Jacob Bobart the Younger, keeper of Oxford's Botanic Gardens, shocked Oxford by producing

Examination Schools' dragon-shaped boot scraper.

the dried corpse of a small dragon. Scientists verified the find, and poets poured forth their astonishment and admiration – at which point Bobart confessed that his dragon was actually the corpse of a rat, its sides stretched with sticks to resemble wings.

In the 1930s, the long-gone Oxford zoo displayed a flying cat looking strangely similar to Bobart's dragon. The poor animal had *cutaneous asthenia*, a disease that causes extreme elasticity of the skin. The 'wings' were 6in long, and the cat was said to use them when pouncing.

The carved Story Tree at Bury Knowle Park in Headington depicts characters from Middle Earth and Narnia, including Tolkien's dragon Smaug from *The Hobbit*. There are some smaller specimens masquerading as boot-scrapers outside the Examination Schools on the High Street.

Giants

John Middleton of Hale in Lancashire, nicknamed 'the Child of Hale', was a seventeenth-century celebrity giant. He is said to have been 9ft 3in (2.8m) tall. His landlord, Sir Gilbert Ireland, was a Brasenose alumnus, and he brought Middleton to Oxford on his way from London, where Middleton had defeated James I's nominated champion in a bout of wrestling. A number of portraits were made of the big man, including the one that still hangs at Brasenose. Middleton also allowed casts of his hand to be made, one of which was viewed for two shillings by freak show fan Samuel Pepys on 9 June 1668: '… to Brazen-nose college; to the butteries, and in the cellar find the hand of the Child of Hales… Oxford mighty fine place, and well seated, and cheap entertainment.'

Pepys was clearly a rich man – two shillings to see a hand print was far from 'cheap entertainment'.

When Brasenose Boat Club was established in 1815, the college boat was named the Child of Hale in Middleton's honour.

Shotover Forest has a legend of a resident giant who 'shot over' various projectiles, hence the name. The round stones found in the local sand are said to be his marbles. The giant was thought to lie in an ancient barrow, 'the Giant's Grave', which sat on the hilltop until it was destroyed by tanks practising for some real shooting in the Second World War. In the seventeenth century a picture of the giant was scratched into the red soil of the hill, wielding bow and arrow; but by 1763 it had disappeared.

Seventeenth-century natural historian Robert Plot concluded that a mysterious specimen he had been sent was the thigh bone of a humanoid giant. Plot ruled out the other leading theory which claimed that it belonged to an elephant – either a victim of one of the menageries that frequently visited the area, or one that had keeled over in the service of the Romans. The bone in reality belongs to Megalosaurus, the first dinosaur to be scientifically described; although that was 150 years after Plot's day.

Giraffe

In the 1850s the Anatomical Museum at Christ Church College was presided over by Henry Acland. As space was limited in the Anatomy School, preparation of museum exhibits was carried out in an adjoining stable. This proved highly offensive to the coachmen and servants who had to endure the terrible odours of rotting animals. It was the giraffe

Oxford coachman.

that tipped them over the edge: the coachmen lodged an official complaint, and before Acland could respond, college servants evicted the offending beast, shovelling it into the middle of the road in St Aldates.

The carcass proved irresistible to one lucky dog, who grabbed the giraffe's tail and bolted. Observant visitors to the University Museum of Natural History will notice that parts of the giraffe exhibit's tail are a different colour to the other bones: they are, in fact, made of lead, replacements for the bits stolen by that opportunistic hound.

Hocus pocus

The word 'hocus-pocus' originated amongst Oxonian wits during the reign of King Edward VI (reigned 1547–53). It was a malicious Protestant parody of *hoc est corpus*, 'this is my body', the words uttered by Catholic priests when handing over the bread during Mass.

Lock-ups

Oxford's lock-ups for petty criminals included a large oak tree at Kidlington. According to seventeenth-century Robert Plot:

> We have [no tree] put to so honourable a use, yet the hollow oak on Kidlington Green, for the necessary and public service it has done… for the imprisoning vagabonds and other mal-efactors for the space of a night or so, till they conveniently might be had to the gaol at Oxford: of whom the hollow is so large within, that it would receive eight or ten commodiously enough, the tree being 25 foot round above the spurs.

The best surviving lock-up hereabouts is the pyrami-dal drunk-tank in Wheatley (a couple of miles east of

Oxford as the U1 bus service flies), a windowless prison designed for maximum sobering-up.

Marriage (or lack of it)

Accepting fellowship of a college carried with it various duties. One of these was to avoid marriage. This ruling began to lapse in the nineteenth century, although some places hung on to bachelorhood and celibacy (not that the former was necessarily tied to the latter) as long as was legally possible. At Wadham it is said that founder Dame Dorothy Wadham fell in love with the institution's first Warden. Her affections were unrequited, and she made the decree of marital abstinence as a type of crossed-lover's revenge.

Mercury Fountain, Christ Church

The pond in Tom Quad at Christ Church (installed 1670) is notable for three disparate phenomena: fish, gods and brawls. The current fish are koi carp, donated by the Empress of Japan in 2007. The god is Mercury, rising above the water in tarnished bronze. The original was installed in 1695, a gift from Dr John Radcliffe, but was stolen in 1817 by the 14th Earl of Derby, Edward Smith-Stanley, a student at the college (and Prime Minister on three separate occasions between 1852 and 1868). The pond had to do without its deity for 111 years, at which point a replacement – a copy of Flemish artist Giovanni de Bologna's 1580 Mercury in Florence – was unveiled, standing proud on a pedestal designed by Sir Edwin Lutyens – one of only two works by the great man in Oxford, the other being Campion Hall (1935–37).

Brawling was one of the university's many sadistic traditional pastimes. From 1670 onwards, the college 'hearties' (students keen on sports) would round up the 'aesthetes' (the arty, non-sporty ones) and throw them into the pond. The most famous dunking was a fictional one – Anthony Blanche in Evelyn Waugh's novel *Brideshead Revisited* is an aesthete who makes the most of the ordeal by larking around in the water: 'I got into the fountain and, you know, it really was most refreshing, so I sported there a little and struck some attitudes, until they turned about and walked sulkily home, and I heard Boy Mulcaster saying, "Anyway, we did put him in Mercury".'

The unsporting behaviour petered out before the Second World War, and these days the college police underline that anyone taking a dip in Mercury's fountain will be 'sconced' (fined).

Punishments

The pillory was used to punish all manner of crimes, from drunkenness and lechery to libel and blasphemy. Playful images of people being pelted with soft mouldy fruit are not the complete story – many people left the pillory with serious, sometimes fatal, injuries. Records of Oxford victims include Edward Clark, condemned for keeping a brothel in 1774; and a man named Tubb – possibly the last pilloried man in Oxford – sentenced in 1810 for perjury and placed in the city's last surviving pillory, on the High Street end of Cornmarket.

In 1577 Roland Jenks was convicted of supporting the Pope by producing illegal Catholic books. He was sentenced to be nailed by the ears to a pillory at Oxford Castle. When he managed to tear himself away he cursed the court that had condemned him. A few days later, two judges, the coroner and several jurors from his trial were dead from typhus, along with others to the total of 300.

High Street.

Alternative punishments for minor offences included the stocks at the butter-bench (formerly at Carfax). These had replaced the old city gallows around 1800. The latter had been colloquially named the Gownsman's Gallows. Magdalen President Dr Martin Routh was recorded as exclaiming: 'What, sir, do you tell me, sir, you never heard of Gownsman's Gallows? Why, I tell you, sir, I have seen two undergraduates hanged on Gownsman's Gallows in Holywell – hanged, sir, for highway robbery.'

Butter Bench, on the right, and Carfax in the eighteenth century.

The whipping cart was another punishment, and although it sounds brutal, it appears that some people escaped lightly. Historian John Richard, writing in the late 1800s, declares: 'it was a practice as useless as it was disgusting, for, as we have learned from one who had himself seen this punishment inflicted, "though dragged the whole length of the Cornmarket and back again, the culprit scarce ever received more than one effective stroke, in consequence of the throng and pressure of the crowd around."'

The same writer asserts: 'Pickpockets, taken in the fact, seldom made their appearance at Sessions, they were usually dragged to the nearest pond or pump, and ducked while any sign of life remained. The same rude justice was extended to those whose religious tenets offended the sovereign mob. Young thieves and minor offenders were usually let off with a thrashing.'

Religious relics

St John's Hospital, the precursor of Magdalen College, had some of the city's best religious relics: Edward the Confessor's comb, a large section of St Bartholomew's skin, and a rib from St Andrew. The comb was said to cure not just bed-head, but headaches. The chief purpose of relics was to advertise a church's pre-eminence, with a mind to getting lots of pilgrims to visit, ogle and part with their small change.

The Reformation disposed of all the city's Catholic-era relics and shrines; although the Tomb of St Frideswide was cobbled together again after the religious storms had subsided, and can be seen in the cathedral chapel at Christ Church.

Sconcing

A sconce is a university term for a fine, inflicted for all manner of perceived offences. The poverty stricken Doctor Samuel Johnson, unable to afford new shoes, was still careless enough to provoke a fine of twopence for missing a lecture (a fine unaltered for at least 400 years prior to Johnson). The event inspired one of the outspoken undergraduate's many famous utterances: 'Sir, you have sconced me twopence for non-attendance on a lecture not worth a penny.'

Sconcing was applied to a wide range of offences. One celebrated Balliol tale tells of a young man who cut his throat in a failed suicide attempt, and was fined five shillings for his efforts. The Master of the college commented drily: 'next time he cuts his throat I'll fine him ten'.

The Skeleton of Giles Covington

In spite of ongoing attempts to have the bones of Giles Covington buried, and to have the man's name cleared by royal pardon, he is still hanging in the former premises of the Museum of Oxford (not on public display, at the time of writing).

Twenty-one-year-old Giles Covington, seaman and petty criminal, had been arrested for the murder of a pedlar after another man suspected of the crime pointed the finger at him in order to gain a royal pardon. Giles protested his innocence throughout the trial, writing contrite and pleading letters from Oxford Prison. But the verdict of guilty was not overturned, and Giles hanged at Oxford on 7 March 1791.

Covington's body was cut down and delivered to Dr Pegge at Christ Church for the Anatomy School. Giles was carved up as the main course at the following day's public lecture. When there was nothing more to be carved, the bones were wired together, and the skeleton became a teaching aid.

In 1860 the bones were displayed in the new University Museum of Natural History on Parks Road. It stood here in its glass case well into the 1960s, with a label which deserves a nomination for Most Useless Museum Label Ever. It read simply, 'Englishman'.

Tossed into the rubbish tip known as the Bone Room, it was only the subtle inscription 'Giles Covington' on the lower jaw bone that saved it. A member of staff did a little research and unearthed the whole sorry tale, and the remains were given to the Museum of Oxford.

Smoking

Smoking was said to have spread to all corners of Oxford society during the civil wars of the seventeenth century, when Royalists and Parliamentarians alike were settled in and around the city for the Siege of Oxford. The chief fashion setters were the German contingent, brought over by Prince Rupert of the Rhine, King Charles I's nephew and commander of the Royal Cavalry. Prior to this the academics of university and church tended not to approve of smoking, and few students seem to have caught the bug.

Oxfordshire's white clay made the ideal tobacco-pipe material, an important factor in embedding the habit in the county. First keeper of the Asholean Museum Robert Plot, writing twenty years after the Civil War, noted, 'At Shotover-hill there is a white clay... which during the late wars, in the siege of Oxford, was wholly used for making Tobacco-pipes there.' The material was generally referred to as 'tobacco pipe clay'. Most gardeners in Oxford will have unearthed a few sections of local clay pipe when turning the soil – they seem to have been discarded as readily as cigarette stubs.

Christ Church.

The Secret History of Oxford

After the wars, and through to the end of the twentieth century via pipe-toting gurus such as J.R.R. Tolkien and C.S. Lewis, no portrait of a man of books was complete without a cloud of pipe smoke.

Tolkien famously mythologised tobacco in his Middle Earth books, making the hobbits and their companions smoke a variety of blends which the author happily detailed in his notes to *The Lord of the Rings*. In a subtle sign of the times, the 2012 movie of *The Hobbit* featured Bilbo Baggins puffing away and producing CGI smoke.

Henry Aldrich, Dean of Christ Church in 1689, writer of the song Bonny Christ Church Bells, composed a Smoking Catch 'to be sung by four men smoking their pipes, not more difficult to sing than diverting to hear.'

Antiquarian and diarist Thomas Hearne (alumnus of St Edmund Hall and one-time assistant Keeper of the Bodleian) recorded a smoking contest in 1723:

At two o'clock in the afternoon was a smoking match over against the theatre, a scaffold being built up for it just at Finmore's, an ale-house. 'Twas thought a journeyman tailor of St Peter's-in-the-East would have been victor, he smoking faster than, and being many pipes before, the rest, but at last he was so sick that 'twas thought he would have died, and an old man that had been a soldier and smoked gently came off conqueror, smoking the three ounces quite out, and four or five pipes the same evening.

The smoking ban of 2006 brought to an end a 360-year-old Oxford habit of smoking; perhaps one of least lamented lost traditions of the city.

Town versus Gown

'Town versus Gown' riots – i.e. Oxford townsfolk versus university students – were not new in 1355; but that year was a watershed, with a conflict that kicked off on St Scholastica's Day, 10 February.

In the Swindlestock Tavern at Carfax a group of students and priests lodged a complaint about the poor

The view of the High Street from Carfax Tower.

quality of the beer. The landlord responded with verbal abuse, and one of the students threw a pot of beer at his head. That was it. Tables went over, fists turned into broken bottles, and then into bows and arrows, knives and cudgels. St Martin's Church bell at Carfax summoned the 'Town' and the bell on the university church of St Mary summoned the 'Gown'.

Site of the now lost Swindlestock Tavern.

The Oxford Mayor called in reinforcements from outside the city – about 2,000 – who advanced chanting, 'Slay, Slay! Havoc, havoc! Smite fast! Give good knocks!'

Some of the university's halls were broken into and in total, over three days, sixty-two students were killed. The Mayor appealed to King Edward III to take the Town's side, but he opted for Gown. The Mayor, his Bailiffs and successors had to attend a Mass for the souls of their dead victims every St Scholastica's Day; and the top section of the church tower at Carfax was knocked down, to prevent the Town from using it as a surrogate castle, as they had in the past.

Even more drastically, the Town had to swear a resurrected oath (first formulated after similar Town versus Gown troubles in 1213) recognising the university's privileges and pre-eminence in the city. They did this each year, and had to go on bended knee to the Vice Chancellor of the university with sixty-two symbolic citizens and hand over sixty-two silver pennies in perpetual compensation. Meanwhile the 'Town and Gown' division was bitter as ever just below the surface

Memory dies hard in Oxford, and this ritual humiliation and 'oneupmanship' was only abolished in 1825. At the 600th anniversary of the St Scholastica's Day riot in 1955 hatchets were finally buried when the Vice-Chancellor gave an honorary degree to the Mayor of Oxford in the Sheldonian Theatre, and in turn was made a Freeman at the Town Hall.

Swindlestock Tavern opened in 1250 and closed in 1709, by which time it had long been known as the Mermaid Tavern. The site of the Tavern is marked with a stone plaque, low down on the wall of Marygold House, currently occupied by Santander Bank.

The earliest recorded Town Versus Gown was in 1209. Riots and retribution had begun when a student killed a

Town versus Gown riot, 1825.

townswoman with an arrow. The townsfolk responded by lynching two students, and the rest fled from the city.

In the 1220s the hard work of Chancellor Grossteste brought order and a new respectability to the restless university. But there were still many riots, as students and townsmen regularly battled it out. 1228 saw one of the bloodiest bouts, with another bloodbath in 1236.

In 1238 the Gown managed to offend the Pope by brawling with the papal legate's party at Osney Abbey.

There were rampages and deaths aplenty in the confrontations of 1252, 1274, 1298 and 1334; and a traditional punch-up on Bonfire Night in November was a fixture of the Oxford calendar until the late nineteenth century.

Turtles

Frank Buckland wrote:

> A live turtle was sent down from London, to be dressed for the banquet in Christ Church Hall [in honour of the Duke of Wellington, 1834]. My father tied a long rope around the turtle's fin, and let him have a swim in "Mercury", the ornamental

water in the middle of the Christ Church "Quad", while I held the string. I recollect, too, that my father made me stand on the back of the turtle while he held me on (I was then a little fellow), and I had a ride for a few yards as it swam round and round the pond. As a treat I was allowed to assist the cook to cut off the turtle's head in the college kitchen. The head, after it was separated, nipped the finger of one of the kitchen boys who was opening the beast's mouth.

Alice 'In Wonderland' Liddell was taken to see the turtles with Lewis Carroll in the college kitchens too. She cried at the starving reptiles' soup-bound fate; and this was the origin of the sad 'mock turtle' in Carroll's *Alice's Adventures in Wonderland*.

Children in general were allowed to ride on the animals prior to their tryst with the chef-cum-executioner, and there are still turtle shells decorating the kitchen walls at the college.

Unicorns

One of the original pre-college university halls in Oxford was called Unicorn, probably named after a coat of arms rather than a relic. The unicorn symbol survives in the heraldic arms of St Hilda's College, founded in 1893. Other city foundations have the genuine article, though.

Amongst the possessions of New College are two unicorn horns. Robert Dudley, Earl of Essex, purloined a section of the oldest one in the sixteenth century, for medicinal purposes. The fellows refused to hand over the entire relic, as originally requested, but granted him a couple of inches. Powdered unicorn horn was said to cure poison (and if that sounds silly, sober up by reflecting on the continuing black market use of rhinoceros horn and other endangered animal parts in the so-called 'medicine' trade). This horn was donated to the college by one of its fellows, William Porte, in 1456, on condition that perpetual prayers should be sung in the college chapel for the safe transit of his soul in the afterlife.

A second, longer horn was donated to New College by the Governor of the Hudson's Bay Company in 1965. He loved the story of Essex and the original horn, and wanted to bolster the unicorn tradition. The 'horns', of course, are not taken from the heads of rare equines. They are narwhal teeth, the narwhal being a member of the whale and dolphin family.

The Anatomy School at Christ Church – one of the fore-runners of the Museum of Natural History – used to have a 'genuine' unicorn horn; whereas the old Ashmolean could only boast a *Unicornu marinum* or 'sea-unicorn' horn (our old friend the narwhal), which was deemed very much second best to the terrestrial variety from a medicinal point of view. The new Ashmolean, however, has perhaps the greatest unicorn treasures of them all – two drawings by Leonardo da Vinci featuring the mythical beast.

University Parks

The University Parks (main entrance off Parks Road) acquired its name from the cannons that were 'parked' here during the Civil War in the seventeenth century. The area was, at the time, a large ploughed field divided by a gravel path, sitting between water meadows and large cottage gardens. Only in the following century did it live up to its name and actually become a park.

War effort

Oxford enjoyed more peacetime in the First World War than the rest of Britain: due to inefficient communications, news of the declaration of war took more than two days to reach Oxford Town Hall.

In the First World War a partition was erected in the grounds of Oriel College, separating the Second and Third Quads. This was to create a self-contained space for the female students of Somerville College, whose building had been appropriated as a military hospital. High-spirited Oriel lads knocked a hole in the wall one night, and until it was repaired, this dangerous conduit was guarded 24/7 by humourless Oriel staff to prevent a scandalous mingling of the sexes.

The Morris car factory at Cowley produced 650 tanks in the Second World War War; while William Morris' sister business the Pressed Steel Company, normally pressing steel car bodies, made its largely female workforce churn out thousands of artillery cartridge cases.

Penicillin was developed in Oxford during the Second World War as the world's first antibiotic. First described by Alexander Fleming in 1925, it was Nazi Germany refugee Ernst Chain and Rhodes Scholar Howard Florey who developed it as a drug fit for mass production. Their guinea pig was an Oxford policeman who was dying from an infected wound inflicted while pruning roses. The drug worked near-miracles; but supplies ran out. Traces were recycled from the policeman's urine, but not enough to save his life.

Bibliography

Books

Boase, Charles William, *Oxford* (Longmans, London, 1887)

Bompas, George. C., *Life of Frank Buckland* (Smith, Elder & Co., London, 1886)

Clark, Sir George, *Oxford and the Civil War* (pamphlet, Oxford, 1970)

Cox, George Valentine, *Recollections of Oxford* (London, 1868)

Craik, George Lillie, *The Pictorial History of England: being a history of the people as well as a history of the Kingdom* (London, 1838)

Ditchfield, P.H. (ed.), *Memorials of Old Oxfordshire* (Bemrose & Sons, London, 1903)

Foxe, John, *The Book of Martyrs* (Foxe's Book of Martyrs), (London, 1563)

Gardiner, Rena, *The Story of Magdalen* (Magdalen College, Oxford, 2003)

Green, John Richard, *Oxford Studies* (Macmillan, London, 1901)

Hogg, Thomas Jefferson, *Shelley at Oxford* (Methuen, London, 1904)

How, Frederick Douglas, *Oxford* (Blackie & Son, London, 1910)

Hutton, Laurence, *Literary Landmarks of Oxford* (Charles Scribner's Sons, New York, 1903)

Ingram, James, *Memorials of Oxford,* three volumes (John Henry Parker, Oxford, 1837)

Jeaffreson, John Cordy, *Annals of Oxford,* two volumes (Hurst and Blackett, London, 1871)

Lang, Andrew, *Oxford* (Seeley, Service & Co., London, 1922)

Morris, Jan, *The Oxford Book of Oxford* (OUP, Oxford, 1978)

Peel, Robert and Minchin, H.C., *Oxford* (Methuen & Co., London, 1905)

Pevsner, Nikolaus and Sherwood, Jennifer, *The Buildings of England: Oxfordshire* (Harmondsworth, London, 1974)

Plot, Robert, *The Natural History of Oxfordshire* (Oxford, 1677)

Quiller-Couch, Lilian M., *Reminiscences of Oxford by Oxford Men* (Clarendon Press, Oxford, 1892)

Smith, Goldwin, *Oxford and her Colleges* (Macmillan & Co., London, 1895)

Bibliography

Spiers, R.A.H., *Round About 'The Mitre' at Oxford (Episodes of the University, City and Hotel)* (The Mitre, Oxford, 1929)

Sullivan, Paul, *Bloody British History: Oxford* (The History Press, Stroud, 2012)

Sullivan, Paul, *The Little Book of Oxfordshire* (The History Press, Stroud, 2012)

Sullivan, Paul, *Oxford: A Pocket Miscellany* (The History Press, Stroud, 2011)

Tuckwell, William, *Reminiscences of Oxford* (Cassell & Co., London, 1901)

Walker, John, *Oxoniana: or Anecdotes Relative to the University and City of Oxford* (Slatter & Munday, Oxford, 1806)

Wells, Joseph, *The Charm of Oxford* (Simpkin, Marshall, Hamilton Kent & Co., London 1921)

Wells, Joseph, *Oxford and Oxford Life* (Methuen & Co., London, 1899)

Whittock, Nathaniel, *Description of the University and City of Oxford...* (Isaac Taylor Hinton, London, 1828)

Wood, Anthony, *Athenæ Oxoniensis* (Ecclesiastical History Society, Oxford, 1848)

Wood, Anthony and Hearne, Thomas, *The Life of Anthony à Wood from the year 1632 to 1672*, (Clarendon Press, Oxford, 1772)

Wood, Anthony, Andrew Clark (ed.), *Survey of the Antiquities of the City of Oxford, composed in 1661-6, by Anthony Wood,* three volumes (Clarendon Press, Oxford, 1889)

Newspapers and journals

Jackson's Oxford Journal (Oxford)
The Oxford Mail (Oxford)
The Oxford Times (Oxford)
Oxford Today (Oxford)
Oxfordshire Limited Edition (Oxford)
Daily Telegraph (London)
The Times (London)
Folklore (London)
Notes & Queries (Oxford)

Websites

www.ashmolean.org
www.british-history.ac.uk
www.headington.org.uk
www.oum.ox.ac.uk
www.ox.ac.uk/colleges
www.oxford.gov.uk

www.oxfordchabad.org
www.oxfordhistory.org.uk/
www.oxfordtimes.co.uk
oxstreets.oxfordcivicsoc.org.uk/
www.shotover.clara.net
en.wikipedia.org

Index of Places

Index of Places

Index of Places

Visit our website and discover thousands of other History Press books.

www.thehistorypress.co.uk